SERIOUS
MISTRANSLATIONS
OF THE BIBLE

SERIOUS MISTRANSLATIONS OF THE BIBLE

By
JACQUES MORE

JAROM BOOKS

To the memory of Dr. Dennis Ball

Dennis – the invited speaker – at a joint church "Come bless the Lord" event held at St. John's Methodist church in Southborough, Kent in September 1982, laid hands on me and prophesied:

"…And as you delve and as you search and as you gain the knowledge of the Word, it shall be the equipment of God being given to you…"

CONTENTS

DOCTRINAL BIAS IN TRANSLATIONS

USE OF NOTES IN TRANSLATIONS

APPENDICES

INTRODUCTION

My first language now is English. It was French. When I became a British subject at 19 I could already converse much better in English than the French with which I began. But the reality that I had to learn English has meant that for me the language is more accurate in transmission than it is fluid. For the written this is more true than the spoken. Accuracy here is more important than fluidity though it is so helpful when both are present. But what I write about is due to the discovery at the age of 14 that there is a living God, and a little later this world also comprised of another entity whom the bible names as the Devil and that his one purpose in life is to deceive the world, I thereby came to hunger and search for truth more than anything. Deception is the one thing that divides God from his creatures and people from each other more than anything else.

There is perhaps no more important a book to know and understand accurately than the bible. It is the one written revelation of God and from him that can tell us what he is like and how to be.

This book is not an exhaustive work on mistranslations of the Bible but a highlighting of numerous passages of importance and interest to the body of

Christ. These are words and passages which I have researched and studied over the years. Some I came only to understand after praying for understanding and trusting the Lord's faithfulness in reply (James 1:5). A few of these discoveries are found in previous books of mine, but this is the first that brings together all the mistranslated that has been learned.

In qualifying the mistranslations as serious I refer to the importance these passages have in this present time in influencing Christians. However I recognise that seriousness is relative, but if this book – The Bible – as the world's undisputed bestseller – is indeed the guide to so many peoples lives, then can even a small error that alters a meaning really not be called serious?

Note on Greek Letters

Where the New Testament Greek is quoted no Greek symbols are used but equivalent English letters as follows:

A-α	Alpha	represented by	*a*
B-β	Bēta	"	*b*
Γ-γ	Gamma	"	*g*
Δ-δ	Delta	"	*d*
E-ε	Epsīlon	"	*e*
Z-ζ	Zēta	"	*dz* or *z*
H-η	Ēta	"	*é*
Θ-θ	Thēta	"	*th*

Ι-ι	Iōta	"	*i*
Κ-κ	Kappa	"	*k*
Λ-λ	Lambda	"	*l*
Μ-μ	Mu	"	*m*
Ν-ν	Nu	"	*n*
Ξ-ξ	Xī	"	*x*
Ο-ο	Omīcron	"	*o*
Π-π	Pī	"	*p*
Ρ-ρ	Rhō	"	*r*
Σ-ς,σ	Sigma	"	*s*
Τ-τ	Tau	"	*t*
Υ-υ	Upsīlon	"	*u*
Φ-φ	Phī	"	*ph*
Χ-χ	Chī	"	*ch*
Ψ-ψ	Psī	"	*ps*
Ω-ω	Ōmega	"	*ó*

In addition to this when the grave accent (`` ` ``) is present over an initial vowel of a word in the Greek: This is represented by "*h*" preceding the word.

A CHAT ABOUT TRANSLATION

Paraphrases – good or bad

When I became a Christian from an un-churched background my access to the bible had been up till then through religious lessons at secondary school – part of the standard curriculum in the UK. The versions used were the Revised Standard Version and the New English Bible. Then, the Gideons on leaving one school gave me a King James Version. But, as these versions were not related to everyday language, when I converted and became aware of the (then) new paraphrase version of the Living Bible I went to my local W H Smith bookshop and bought my 1st bible. It felt special to buy this 1st copy of the Word of God for myself. This was a thick paperback (over 5cm) version of Dr Kenneth Taylor's famous Living Bible translation and before too long required multiple attempts at repair with sellotape and became multicoloured in the many underlined passages.

A paraphrase version of the bible then is an ideal version to use as a readable, accessible version for the purpose of getting familiar with the contents of the bible. It is a great way to relate concepts and ideas in every day language.

But a paraphrase is not an accurate translation. Now the bible text in the original languages is understood as inspired just as Paul wrote here:

> All Scripture *is* given by inspiration of God, and *is* profitable for doctrine, for reproof, for correction, for instruction in righteousness, that the man of God may be complete, thoroughly equipped for every good work.   *2 Timothy 3:16-17*

Literally the Greek word *theopneustos* means "God breathed". In the quote, translated in the default translation used in this book – the New King James Version (NKJV) – it is translated "inspiration of God".

Note: Where words are not found in the Greek, and in this quote this is the verb "*is*" the NKJV places the word in italics to show that it has been added. This is a helpful aid in a version that seeks to be accurate in relating the meaning as literally as possible.

Now, if the Scripture is God breathed then when it comes to doctrine and teaching that affects the way we think of God or treat each other, then I believe a direct and more literal translation is more preferable than a paraphrase. This is especially true if a series of texts are used to make a point or build up a teaching. But for general understanding, for inspiration and, occasionally specifics, a paraphrase is good. After all, Jesus and Paul quoted the paraphrase of their day as testified in our very bibles. I explain this in the following chapter. So by this very example of Jesus and the apostles' use of the paraphrase of their day, we have a help in giving value to today's paraphrases.

However, it is needful for the bible teacher and pastor to be conscious that just as Jesus uses the Scripture specifically into an issue by quoting it accurately against the devil when he was tempted in the wilderness, who himself was quoting it to tempt Jesus, so an accurate reading of the God-breathed is needed to counteract the lies and deceit of the evil one. A paraphrase is easier to get waylaid from the truth than a literal version.

But, it is not helpful when a version claims to be a literal or direct translation when in reality many portions are paraphrased. I would not be the first to say that the NIV is more a paraphrase in places than a direct translation. So, if in doubt or in wishing to study a text it is good and common practise to read a number of versions. But, no matter how little of the original language is known or understood I have found even more of the flavour of the original is appreciated with an interlinear. Even if just the English words in the interlinear are followed: Sometimes the very order of the words helps to gain something more out of the passage in view.

Let's now take a look at an oft forgotten source that can help us return to understanding the bible more accurately.

INCORRECT WORD MEANINGS

3

INCORRECT WORD MEANINGS

In this section of chapters about particular Greek words being mistranslated 4 particular Greek words will be looked at:

EKLEKTOS
SUNEKLEKTOS
GENEA
TASSÓ (as it affects Acts 13:48)

The first three in particular are (in the main) examples where the word meaning has been lost due to lack of use of the language and reliance on a select group of lexicons – word dictionaries – which themselves miss out on an important source of information. That is to say as Greek use went out of norm in the 4th and 5th centuries in the world of the day, Latin then took over as the lingua franca between academics, traders and national administrations. Lingua franca is the term used for the main language that is used as the common bridge to communicate for commerce, administration and intellectual exchanges when many countries have their own different languages within a region that accommodates many countries. The modern example of that is how English is used today in all the world of aviation.

In this section of chapters about particular Greek words being mistranslated the Septuagint will be used as a valuable source to discover a better rendering. It is a valuable source for meaning of words that has been neglected or little considered by lexicons.

The Septuagint

The bible of Jesus' day was the Old Testament of our bibles. This bible existed mainly in two languages, the original Hebrew – a few portions of that version are in Aramaic, namely in Daniel and Ezra – and the other language is the Greek translation that is now known as the Septuagint (LXX). The name Septuagint is based on the historical record that 70 + 2 scholars did the work of that translation. This was at the request of Ptolemy II Philadelphus to the high priest Eleazar in Israel to send 6 elders out of each tribe to the work of translating the Hebrew law of the Jews which dates the work during the reign between 283–246BC. Josephus the historian records all this in his 12th book of Antiquities Chapter 2 sections 4–7 which he wrote about 94AD. The Antiquities also mention the law containing wisdom (section 4) and it may be understood thereby that more than just the 5 books of the law was translated into Greek. This view would be supported by the clear request for all possible explanation of these things to be given, so any book other than Moses' available and part of the Jewish canon is likely to have been included in that translation work. Josephus takes great care to describe in detail the gifts given to Eleazar the high priest and the temple but the law he mentions as if complete so that it appears safer to suggest all the known canon was included in his meaning. Josephus in his accurate rendering of the story is unlikely to have omitted a mention that anything was not translated if he knew of this. It is of equal note that when Paul talks of "the law" as in Romans 3:19 for example, he is actually referring to the Psalms and other passages not written by Moses and which he quoted in the preceding verses of Romans 3. With Moses known as the writer of the first 5 books of the Old Testament and these named as the books of the law, some have thought the Septuagint was only about these books at the beginning. This is because when Josephus mentions the law as to be translated some assume this only means the books of Moses. Paul's very practise of using "the law" to mean other books of the Old Testament indicates this was not the understanding of the day.

Now we know the world of books in the Middle East and Europe consisted of hand written works until the full introduction of printing for the written word in the 15th century. And we know that we have more attestation to the origin of the New Testament copies than we have of the Septuagint copies. However, the very quotes of Jesus and Paul which are identical to the later extant versions of the Septuagint attest to the existence of a translation in Greek already there to be quoted as well as thereby the lesser use of the Hebrew in teaching and reading in the synagogues by the time of Jesus' day. The New Testament itself thus points to the validity of this translation of the Old Testament. Now, I am not referring to any inspiration of the translation, but to its existence and its usefulness in appreciating the meaning of Greek words in the New Testament Greek. It is this latter use that I wish to highlight. The fact that the New Testament was written in the same language as the LXX makes it an invaluable resource to appreciate the words in the New Testament. It is like a Rosetta stone when compared with the Hebrew text from which it was translated.

The above is my thinking in regards to the Septuagint and replies to modern objections of the usefulness or reliability of the Septuagint.

Jesus and the apostles quote the LXX
Matthew 4:10
Jesus said to the Devil in the wilderness:

> Away with you, Satan! For it is written, *'You shall worship the* LORD *your God, and Him only you shall serve.'* Matthew 4:10

Initial note: The italics in this passage are to show this is a quote from the Old Testament. This is the other use of italics in the NKJV.

The Septuagint contains the words *kai autó monó* in English "and Him only", and this "only" translated from Deuteronomy 6:13 is not found in the Hebrew. Because our Old Testament is translated from the original Hebrew it is why the word "only" cannot be read in the Old Testament passage. As we can see:

> You shall fear the LORD your God and serve Him, and shall take oaths in His name.   *Deuteronomy 6:13*

The word "only" is not there. This vouches therefore for Matthew and Jesus' use of the Septuagint as it does Luke who quotes Jesus saying the same thing against the Devil in Luke 4:8 "**and Him only you shall you serve**".

Matthew 15:8-9

> *'These people draw near to Me with their mouth, and honor Me with their lips, but their heart is far from Me. And in vain they worship Me, teaching as doctrines the commandments of men.'*
>
> *Matthew 15:8-9*

Here is a quote by Jesus primarily of Isaiah 29:13. Similar sentiments are found in Psalm 78:36-37 and Ezekiel 33:31. The Hebrew does not contain "***in vain they worship Me***" whilst it is there in the Septuagint: *matén de debontai me.*

John
John quotes Isaiah 53:1 like this:

> *'Lord, who has believed our report? And to whom*
> *has the arm of the LORD been revealed?'* *John 12:38*

The translated Hebrew version in our bibles has:

> Who has believed our report? And to whom has the
> arm of the LORD been revealed?   *Isaiah 53:1*

The passage begins without "Lord" in the Hebrew; it
is there in the LXX which John is quoting.

Paul

A good example of Paul's use of the LXX:

> Beloved, do not avenge yourselves, but *rather* give
> place to wrath; for it is written, *'Vengeance is Mine,*
> *I will repay,'* says the Lord. *'Therefore if your enemy*
> *hungers, feed him; if he thirsts, give him a drink;*
> *for in so doing you will heap coals of fire on his*
> *head.'*   *Romans 12:19-20*

This latter OT quote is direct from Proverbs 25:21-22.
The Greek is exactly the same in the Septuagint as the
New Testament Text. Whilst in the Hebrew Text and
our Bibles Proverbs 25:21-22 reads,

> If your enemy is hungry, give him bread to eat; and
> if he is thirsty, give him water to drink; for *so* you
> will heap coals of fire on his head . . .
>   *Proverbs 25:21-22*

16

Paul makes no mention of "bread" or "water" but it is clearly there in the Hebrew. Equally he mentions "in so doing" which is in the Septuagint and nowhere in the Hebrew. This common use of the Septuagint by the New Testament writers makes it a valuable resource for appreciating the meaning of words in the language of the New Testament.

Peter

A good example of Peter's use of the LXX:

> *All flesh is as grass, and all the glory of man as the flower of the grass. The grass withers, and its flower falls away, but the word of the LORD endures forever.*   *1 Peter 1:24-25*

This is a quote of Isaiah 40:6-8. In our bibles translated from the Hebrew this reads,

> All flesh *is* grass, and all its loveliness *is* like the flower of the field. The grass withers, the flower fades, because the breath of the LORD blows upon it; surely the people *are* grass. The grass withers, the flower fades, but the word of our God stands forever.
> *Isaiah 40:6-8*

Peter's quoting is not as accurate as Paul's was, but the main sections are identical to the LXX. The LXX translation of Isaiah and Peter's quote make no mention of "**the breath of the Lord blows upon it**". Equally the LXX and Peter mention "**the glory of man**"

17

which is not in the Hebrew. Interestingly Peter ends with "**the word of the Lord**" – I did say his quoting was not so accurate – whereas both the LXX and the Hebrew have "**the word of our God**".

Use of the Septuagint

If a word can be clearly shown to have an emphasis in the LXX different than has up till now been used in the N.T. we should take notice. It is not about the accuracy of translation of the LXX or indeed any claim on inspiration given to it that is the value given here; it is the recognition that it was known and used by the Lord and his apostles that makes it worth taking note of in regards to the use of words in the same language as used to write the New Testament.

4

EKLEKTOS

Sometime in the 1990s I read Roger Forster and Paul Marston's book *God's strategy in human history*. I was surprised to read that in the Septuagint (LXX) the word *eklektos* was identified as meaning "quality" with an example given. I thought if this was true it was important to check out. So I called up the manager of a local Christian Bookshop I knew and asked if he could get hold of a copy of the LXX. He told me that he just "happened" to have one in stock, as someone had ordered it but not collected it. He then asked me if I "happened" to want a copy of the concordance too!

The word *eklektos* is found 23 times in the New Testament (NT) where it is seen translated as "elect" and "chosen". So if quality is what is meant then this is significant.

Eklektos is in Matthew 20:16 (See N.B.); 22:14; 24:22; 24:24; 24:31. It is in Mark 13:20; 13:22; 13:27. It is in Luke 18:7; 23:35. It is in Paul's letters: Romans 8:33; 16:13; Colossians 3:12; 1 Timothy 5:21; 2 Timothy 2:10; Titus 1:1. It is in Peter's letters 1 Peter 1:2 (Gk: 1:1); 2:4; 2:6; 2:9. And it is in John's letters and the final book in the bible: 2 John 1; 2 John 13; Revelation 17:14.

Note: Matthew 20:16 does not contain this portion in the Greek Text used for the translation of many modern versions.

Now, since the LXX is a translation of the Hebrew OT into the same language as the NT, then a word found in both gives us the LXX as a valuable means of recognising what a word meant in the NT. A look at what Hebrew words are translated into *eklektos* gives us the flavour of that word when there are sufficient examples to do so. This is clearly so as regards *eklektos*.

The word *eklektos* is found 82 times in the LXX of which 7 are sections of the translation which have no counterpart passages in the Old Testament (OT) Hebrew text. This leaves us with 75 to look at, but for the full list see Appendix 1.

There are 52 examples of *eklektos* in the LXX which give an overwhelming picture of the emphasis of quality.

There are 23 examples of *eklektos* in the LXX to translate Hebrew words which are known for "chosen" (18); "elect" (4); "choose" (1) in the KJV. These Hebrew words are elsewhere seen in the LXX as not translated as *eklektos* and one as only translated by *eklektos*. This indicates that in these few places the LXX translators did not recognise the emphasis of "a selection" as involved, but something closer to the clear picture elsewhere – see Appendix 1 for an analysis of the Hebrew words. So what is this clear picture?

Well, before I go there, I wish to highlight where the current emphasis in the New Testament of "elect" and "chosen" has difficulties. Of the 23 passages with *eklektos* in the NT one is about angels:

> I charge *you* before God and the Lord Jesus Christ and the elect angels that you observe these things without prejudice, doing nothing with partiality.
> *1 Timothy 5:21*

This use of "elect" for angels brings up interesting questions:

> Did God select angels?
> Did God make the other angels rebel?
> Did God want angels to rebel?

Of the 23 passages 3 are about Jesus:

> . . . He saved others; let Him save Himself if He is the Christ, the chosen of God.   *Luke 23:35*

> Coming to Him *as to* a living stone, rejected indeed by men, but chosen by God *and* precious . . .
> *1 Peter 2:4*

> *Behold, I lay in Zion a chief cornerstone, elect, precious, and he who believes on Him will by no means be put to shame.*   *1 Peter 2:6*

21

Was Jesus really selected?
Was Jesus picked from among others?

So, what is the clear picture given by the LXX?
Here is a good selection:

Seven cows . . . **fat** [**fat**fleshed KJV]	Genesis 41:2
Seven heads of grain . . . **plump**	Genesis 41:5
choice chariots [**the best** NIV]	Exodus 14:7
quality spices [**pure** myrrh KJV]	Exodus 30:23
With the **pure** . . . Yourself **pure**	2 Samuel 22:27
Fatted oxen . . . **fatted** fowl	1 kings 4:23
Young men* (guys in their prime)	2 Kings 8:12 (*often)
Clear as the sun	Song of Solomon 6:10
A **tried** stone	Isaiah 28:16
Precious stones	Isaiah 54:12
The **highest** branches	Ezekiel 17:22
The **Desire** of All Nations	Haggai 2:7
Pleasant land	Zechariah 7:14

In Pharaoh's dream that Joseph interpreted a contrast between emaciated cows and fat fleshed quality cattle is made. The emphasis that prime and quality beef is in view is given by *eklektos*.

The best chariots and young men – guys in their physical prime – are seen as the best of their kind by *eklektos*.

The highest branches, the most desired country, the quality of solid tried stone, the clarity of the sun, with the pure You will show Yourself pure, all are expressed by *eklektos*.

There is an overwhelming and clear recognition by these that *eklektos* is about QUALITY.

This is the clear testimony of the Scripture text quoted regularly by Jesus and the apostles.

So that, with "quality" in mind with words like "pure", "tried", "fit", what do you think of Jesus' following words?

> Many are called, but few *eklektos*.
>
> *Matthew 20:16 & 22:14*

Is it not better recognised as: "few are fit" or, "few are up to the task"?

This is why I translate this as,

> . . . for many are called, but few *have* mettle.
>
> *Matthew 20:16 & 22:14 JM*

So, was Jesus selected?
Or, is He Special?
Were angels picked out?
Or, are they "the good ones"?

Answer: The evidence from the LXX points to the latter.

How would you say "chosen"?
But, if you were a Greek speaker or writer and you wanted to say this person or that thing is "chosen", how would you say it?

Answer 1: You would use the Greek word for that – *eklogé*

> But the Lord said to him, "Go, for he is a chosen
> vessel of Mine to bear My name before Gentiles, kings,
> and the children of Israel. For I will show him how
> many things he must suffer for My name's sake."
>
> *Acts 9:15-16*

Here Paul is spoken of by the Lord to Ananias and he is described as "chosen" for a purpose. However, this word is mostly translated as "election" so that literally this verse says that Paul is a vessel of election. It is translated as "election" in Romans 9:11; 11:5; 11:7; 11:28; 1 Thessalonians1:4 and 2 Peter 1:10.

Answer 2: You would use the verb for that – *eklegó/ eklegomai*

> . . . until the day in which He was taken up, after He
> through the Holy Spirit had given commandments
> to the apostles whom He had chosen . . .   *Acts 1:2*

> Then it pleased the apostles and elders, with
> the whole church, to send chosen men of their
> own company to Antioch with Paul and Barnabas,
> *namely*, Judas who was also named Barsabas, and
> Silas, leading men among the brethren   *Acts 15:22*

> It seemed good to us, being assembled with one
> accord, to send chosen men to you with our beloved
> Barnabas and Paul,   *Acts 15:25*

> But God has chosen the foolish things of the world to
> put to shame the wise, and God has chosen the weak

24

things of the world to put to shame the things which
are mighty . . .   *1 Corinthians 1:27*

. . . just as He chose us in Him before the foundation
of the world, that we should be holy and without
blame before Him in love . . .   *Ephesians 1:4*

Remaining examples for this verb are Mark 13:20;
Luke 6:13; 10:42; 14:7; John 6:70; 13:18; 15:16;
15:19; Acts 1:24; 6:5; 13:17; 15:7; 1 Corinthians
1:28 and James 2:5

Answer 3: You would use the verb for that – *hairetizó*

Behold! My Servant whom I have chosen, My
Beloved in whom My soul is well pleased: I will
put My Spirit upon Him, and He will declare
justice to the Gentiles.   *Matthew 12:18*

This is the only example in the NT. Both the above
verbs are common in the LXX and here is an example
where the Hebrew translated into English shows the
verb "to choose" is twice in a verse where in the LXX
the 1st is translated by *eklegó* and the 2nd by *hairetizô*:

However the LORD God of Israel chose me above all
the house of my father to be king over Israel forever,
for He has chosen Judah *to be* the ruler. And of the
house of Judah, the house of my father, and among
the sons of my father, He was pleased with me to
make *me* king over all Israel.   *1 Chronicles 28:4*

Answer 4: You would use the verb for that – *haireó/ haireomai*

> But we are bound to give thanks to God always for you, brethren beloved by the Lord, because God from the beginning chose you for salvation through sanctification by the Spirit and belief in the truth,
> *2 Thessalonians 2:13*

The remaining examples for this verb in the NT are Philippians 1:22 and Hebrews 11:25. This is also common in the LXX.

Answer 5: You would use any of the following lesser used verbs for that: *epilegó, procherizomai, cheirotoneó, procheirotoneó, stratologeó*

> . . . but Paul chose Silas and departed, being commended by the brethren to the grace of God.
> *Acts 15:40*

This is the only example in the NT for *epilegó*. It is more common in the LXX. Less common and equally with only 1 example in the NT are *procherizomai* in Acts 22:14, *cheirotoneó* in 2 Corinthians 8:19, *procheirotoneó* in Acts 10:41 and *stratologeó* in 2 Timothy 2:4.

Why has the meaning of *eklektos* been lost?

The honest answer would be to say I don't know: Not specifically anyway. But, there are a number of pointers to what may be the cause. The Septuagint appears to have been missed or discarded as a valuable source for evidence of the meaning of words.

In the late 4th century Jerome a scholar in the three languages, Hebrew, Greek and Latin was asked by the current pope to put together an official translation of the Scriptures into Latin which was by then the most common tongue for administration and commerce in the Roman Empire. At first he translated the LXX into Latin, but progressively he discovered that the LXX translation was not as accurate and more of a paraphrase of the Hebrew text of the OT than was desired for accuracy. So that he is one of the first to depart from the LXX as the source of the OT reading for the early church. This was a good thing as far as the reading of the OT was concerned, but as far as the use of Greek words is concerned and thereby the usefulness of the LXX in that respect, perhaps this lessening in the importance of the LXX was a beginning and a cause for later scholars reasoning for overlooking the LXX.

Now Augustine of Hippo corresponded abundantly with Jerome and is recognised as the departing point from previous early church writers as regards free will. He began the "free will is not" teaching in the church and thus all unconditional predestination dogma as regards salvation for individual believers has its foundation in Augustine's Writings. I demonstrate that with a multitude of quotes from early church writers and compilers of the history of doctrine in my book *So you think you're chosen?* (As did Forster and Marston before me).

It is recognised that the New Testament was not completed into Latin by Jerome for the translation that was later to be named the Latin Vulgate. This version then became the most influential translation of the bible up to the 16th century reformation. From that point on arose the Protestant and other denominations and new versions came about into the more common tongues of the nations in Europe and not least of these was the King James Version. Could it be that Augustine influenced the Vulgate in the New Testament as it was being completed with regards to his new doctrine?

As the reformation began and what is now commonly called Calvinism – Augustine's new teaching retold – took hold as the dominant theology, Beza – John Calvin's successor – became the source of the Greek text changes for the KJV. This influence then readily attested in the history of the KJV translation is the reason this doctrinal variation in the translation of the bible was maintained in the KJV and this has further influenced other versions where departure from the norm or the familiar is regularly avoided.

It has not been since the end of the 19th century that attempts at new translation work – irrespective of the old or new source of Greek texts for translating – began to take place, but still the LXX appears to have been overlooked as a valuable source for the meaning of Greek words. So much so that Greek word dictionaries aplenty omit the LXX evidence and contradict it. So the full and particular reason why, I cannot give, but I trust some possible indicators have been given.

Who are the elect?

Robert Young who thoroughly studied every word in the Greek and the Hebrew for his concordance of the bible also translated a literal version. He included in his introduction to the NT a section about reading differently words found in his translation:

| *For* Elect | *Read* choice one |
| *For* Chosen | *Read* choice one |

He entitled the section "Explanation of 100 bible terms". His view then is not to see "selection" in those words in the NT but "quality".

So how should we translate *eklektos*?

In view of the above when you read of "the elect" or "the chosen" in a bible, then think of these:

"The good guys", "the righteous", "the faithful", "the saints", "the steadfast", for there is better seen a quality emphasis.

So let's see a better translation for the 23 NT passages affected remembering the default translation in this book is the NKJV for the unmentioned source of bible reference.

Matthew 20:16

Where we find,

> . . . For many are called, but few chosen.
>
> *Matthew 20:16*

As we saw, this becomes.

> . . . For many are called, but few *have* mettle.
> *Matthew 20:16 JM*

See note at the beginning of the chapter as regards this text not being found in later bible versions.

Matthew 22:14
Equally we find,

> For many are called, but few *are* chosen.
> *Matthew 22:14*

This then is also,

> For many are called, but few *have* mettle.
> *Matthew 22:14 JM*

Matthew 24:22
Where we read,

> And unless those days were shortened, no flesh would be saved; but for the elect's sake those days will be shortened. *Matthew 24:22*

This is more clearly understood with,

> And unless those days were shortened, no flesh would be saved; but for the righteous' sake those days will be shortened. *Matthew 24:22 JM*

Mark 13:20

Equally in the parallel passage in Mark,

> And unless the Lord had shortened those days, no
> flesh would be saved; but for the elect's sake, whom
> He chose, He shortened the days.   *Mark 13:20*

Now, since "chosen" and "elect" are interchangeable, a
reason "elect" has been used here rather than "chosen"
is that it would be odd and strange looking to read
"for the chosen's sake, whom He chose". If they are
"chosen" then why repeat the fact? But, if *eklektos* is
about quality – as is manifest – then the passage is
about the good guys whom the Lord chose to go
through those days. And it is for their sake that the
days are shortened: the time is limited for them to
be patient and endure the suffering season. So here
we need,

> And unless the Lord had shortened those days, no
> flesh would be saved; but for the righteous' sake, whom
> He chose, He shortened the days.   *Mark 13:20 JM*

Matthew 24:24

Since "quality" is better pictured in English with
"the righteous" then with "the saints" I used it in
Mark 13:20, but here to help focus on the believing
individuals involved "the saints" is suitable.

> For false Christs and false prophets will arise and show great signs and wonders, so as to deceive, if possible, even the elect.   *Matthew 24:24*

This would then become,

> For false Christs and false prophets will arise and show great signs and wonders, so as to deceive, if possible, even the saints.   *Matthew 24:24 JM*

Mark 13:22

This is equally valid for this parallel text,

> For false christs and false prophets will rise and show signs and wonders to deceive, if possible, even the elect.   *Mark 13:22*

Which like Matthew 24:24 above then becomes,

> For false christs and false prophets will rise and show signs and wonders to deceive, if possible, even the saints.   *Mark 13:22 JM*

Matthew 24:31

This use of "saints" in English is seen again as appropriate here, though "His righteous" or "His righteous ones" could work dependent on the desired flow of the translator:

> And He will send His angels with a great sound of a
> trumpet, and they will gather together His elect from
> the four winds, from one end of heaven to the other.
> *Matthew 24:31*

This then becomes,

> And He will send His angels with a great sound of
> a trumpet, and they will gather together His saints
> from the four winds, from one end of heaven to the
> other. *Matthew 24:31 JM*

Mark 13:27

As per the parallel passage of Matthew 24:31 it is also
here,

> And then He will send His angels, and gather together
> His elect from the four winds, from the farthest part
> of earth to the farthest part of heaven. *Mark 13:27*

Then becomes,

> And then He will send His angels, and gather together
> His saints from the four winds, from the farthest part of
> earth to the farthest part of heaven. *Mark 13:27 JM*

Luke 18:7

Remember it is "quality" that is the emphasis so any
word that helps bring that out is useful and I use here
"faithful" to show this,

> And shall God not avenge His own elect who cry out
> day and night to Him, though He bears long with
> them? *Luke 18:7*

This then becomes,

> And shall God not avenge His own faithful who cry
> out day and night to Him, though He bears long
> with them? *Luke 18:7 JM*

Luke 23:35

Here in the sense of "the special one" the words
"the anointed" serve sufficiently to remove a selection
emphasis. Bearing in mind this is a quoted sneer or
sarcastic remark it works to show the intended special-
ness and uniqueness of Jesus,

> And the people stood looking on. But even the rulers
> with them sneered, saying, "He saved others; let Him
> save Himself if He is the Christ, the chosen of God."
> *Luke 23:35*

Then becomes,

> And the people stood looking on. But even the
> rulers with them sneered, saying, "He saved others;
> let Him save Himself if He is the Christ, the anointed
> of God." *Luke 23:35 JM*

Romans 8:33

Here in English the word "saints" or "faithful" serve well. Even though these are normally translations of their own separate Greek word counterparts, it is only the lack of an English equivalent to say "the quality ones" that asks for their use.

> Who shall bring a charge against God's elect? *It is* God who justifies. *Romans 8:33*

This then becomes,

> Who shall bring a charge against God's saints? God *is* the righteous declarer. *Romans 8:33 JM*

Romans 16:13

The same applies here,

> Greet Rufus, chosen in the Lord, and his mother and mine. *Romans 16:13*

This then becomes,

> Greet Rufus, faithful in the Lord, and his mother and mine. *Romans 16:13 JM*

Colossians 3:12

The same applies here,

> Therefore, as the elect of God, holy and beloved, put on tender mercies, kindness, humbleness of mind, meekness, longsuffering . . . *Colossians 3:12*

This then becomes,

> Therefore, as the faithful of God, holy and beloved, put on tender mercies, kindness, humility, meekness, longsuffering . . . *Colossians 3:12 JM*

1 Timothy 5:21

Here a contrast is made between the two types of angels that exist: the fallen and wicked ones in contrast to those that remained at God's side from the beginning, so "good" ones as opposed to the "bad" ones serves well,

> I charge *you* before God and the Lord Jesus Christ and the elect angels that you observe these things without prejudice, doing nothing with partiality.
> *1 Timothy 5:21*

This then becomes,

> I charge you before God and the Lord Jesus Christ and the good angels that you observe these things without prejudice, doing nothing with partiality.
> *1 Timothy 5:21 JM*

2 Timothy 2:10

As we know from above quality is the emphasis for *eklektos* and in view of the purpose Paul mentions in this verse I think it best to use "the righteous" more than "the saints" to translate *eklektos*, as the latter tends to be more used for those already Christians. And here when I read of "the righteous" I think of all like Cornelius of whom Peter said **"In truth I perceive that God shows no partiality. But in every nation whoever fears Him and works righteousness is accepted by Him."** (Acts 10:34-35). These then also need to hear the good news about Jesus that they may obtain assurance of salvation. So that the verse,

> Therefore I endure all things for the sake of the elect, that they also may obtain the salvation which is in Christ Jesus with eternal glory.   *2 Timothy 2:10*

Then becomes,

> Therefore I endure all things for the sake of the righteous, that they also may obtain the salvation which is in Christ Jesus with eternal glory.
> *2 Timothy 2:10 JM*

Titus 1:1

Here Paul introduces himself and his ministry to which he was called in sharing God's eternal purpose of everlasting life for the godly.

> Paul, a servant of God and an apostle of Jesus
> Christ, according to the faith of God's elect and the
> acknowledgment of the truth which is according to
> godliness, in hope of eternal life which God, who
> cannot lie, promised before time began . . .
>
> *Titus 1:1-2*

In view of the truth relating to the godly or pious i.e.
of all times, the righteous as opposed to the wicked, as
two distinct groups are those seen throughout history
in Scripture: the "righteous" emphasis then serves well
more than "the saints" (cf. Romans 2:6-16).

> Paul, servant of God and apostle of Jesus Christ,
> according to the faith of God's righteous and
> knowledge of the truth which is according to piety
> upon hope of eternal life, which the un-lying God
> promised before the ages of time . . . *Titus 1:1-2 JM*

1 Peter 1:1-2

Here it is helpful to note the order of the words in the
Greek. A quick way to do that is quote Young's literal
translation:

> Peter, an apostle of Jesus Christ, to the choice
> sojourners of the dispersion of Pontus, Galatia,
> Cappadocia, Asia, and Bithynia, according to a fore-
> knowledge of God the Father, in sanctification of the
> Spirit, to obedience and sprinkling of the blood of
> Jesus Christ: Grace to you and peace be multiplied!
>
> *1 Peter 1:1-2 Young*

This helps take note of the deliberate re-ordering of the words apparent to provide assistance to the idea of unconditional election as discussed in the chapters on doctrinal bias in translations: see especially the chapter *Such as should be saved.* The idea that there is an elect group – chosen and decided by God is not in view in the text: But appears that way when reading "**elect according to the foreknowledge of God the Father**".

> Peter, an apostle of Jesus Christ,
> To the pilgrims of the Dispersion in Pontus, Galatia, Cappadocia, Asia, and Bithynia, elect according to the foreknowledge of God the Father, in sanctification of the Spirit, for obedience and sprinkling of the blood of Jesus Christ:
> Grace to you and peace be multiplied.   *1 Peter 1:1-2*

If the actual order of the words are recognised and that it is not needful by manipulation to re-order them to assist any recognised grammatical relationship, then all Peter is highlighting in the words "**foreknowledge of God the Father, in sanctification of the Spirit, to obedience and sprinkling of the blood of Jesus Christ**" is that his introduction as an apostle and what that sending – apostle is someone sent – is about: the good news of salvation in Jesus, this highlight then is of that gospel which was foreknown and is part of his introduction in his letter.

To the question "What was foreknown?" the answer is: the good news of the sanctification of the

39

Spirit into obedience and sprinkling of the blood of Jesus, i.e. the good news about Jesus of late declared and at the core of his apostleship was foreknown, as was now revealed at this time.

So as far as *eklektos* is concerned this passage has the "faithful" in view and this is a good word to use.

> Peter, an apostle of Jesus Christ, to the faithful pilgrims of the dispersion of Pontus, Galatia, Cappadocia, Asia, and Bithynia, according to a foreknowledge of God the Father, in sanctification of the Spirit, to obedience and sprinkling of the blood of Jesus Christ: Grace to you and peace be multiplied! *1 Peter 1:1-2 JM*

1 Peter 2:4

Young's is useful here too to show the quality meaning as it is self evident from the Person in view not being chosen from among others, but being the only begotten Son of God: Jesus.

> . . . to whom coming – a living stone – by men, indeed, having been disapproved of, but with God choice, precious . . . *1 Peter 2:4 Young*

So that,

> Coming to Him *as to* a living stone, rejected indeed by men, but chosen by God *and* precious . . .
> *1 Peter 2:4*

Then becomes,

> Coming to Him *as to* a living stone, rejected indeed
> by men, but with God fit, precious . . . *1 Peter 2:4 JM*

The ongoing challenge is to use an appropriate English word to show quality which is the emphasis of the word and indeed the passage as it is a comparison between the worthlessness view in the rejection of men and that of the worthiness seen by God: a rejected stone by men, but one wholly fit for purpose to God. There is no single English word that comes really close to *eklektos* to show quality. Perhaps the nearest in English is as per Matthew 20:16 and 22:14 above, where "*to have* mettle" was used. As you see Young uses the word "choice" which gives that emphasis. So "fit" is good.

1 Peter 2:6

This is a continuation of the theme in Verse 4 and the same thinking applies. So that,

> *Behold, I lay in Zion a chief cornerstone, elect,*
> *precious, and he who believes on Him will by no*
> *means be put to shame.*   *1 Peter 2:6*

The italics here are the practise of the NKJV version to show this is quote from the Old Testament of Isaiah 28:16 which says:

> Therefore thus says the Lord GOD:
> "Behold, I lay in Zion a stone for a foundation, a tried stone, a precious cornerstone, a sure foundation; whoever believes will not act hastily."   *Isaiah 28:16*

1 Peter 2:6 then becomes,

> *Behold, I lay in Zion a chief cornerstone, fit, precious, and he who believes on Him will by no means be put to shame.*   *1 Peter 2:6 JM*

It is of note that no idea of selection: "chosen" or "elect" is in the Old Testament Scripture whatsoever.

1 Peter 2:9

Continuing the theme that Jesus is special and quality is seen in him, but now his followers are in view in contrast to unbelievers – those offended at Him, Peter says that believers are not like these offended, but also are of quality like Jesus. Again Young shows this well.

> And ye *are* a choice race, a royal priesthood, a holy nation, a people acquired, that the excellences ye may shew forth of Him who out of darkness did call you to His wondrous light;   *1 Peter 2:9 Young*

So that this Verse:

> But you *are* a chosen generation, a royal priesthood, a holy nation, His own special people, that you may

> proclaim the praises of Him who called you out of
> darkness into His marvellous light;   *1 Peter 2:9*

Then becomes "**a choice race**" in Young: There is a choice as to what words are best to use to show the quality emphasis. As we see Young uses the word "choice" for quality and "race" rather than "generation" – see the chapter on *genea* in regards to "generation" – I like "faithful family" as the family/related group is in view as per the "race" and the emphasis in quality is as a contrast to the preceding "unbelieving" who stumble at the rock of Jesus.

> But you are a faithful family, a royal priesthood, a
> holy nation, His own special people, that you may
> proclaim the praises of Him who called you out of
> darkness into His marvellous light;   *1 Peter 2:9 JM*

2 John 1

The Greek for "Lord" is *kurios* and the female counterpart *kuria* is found in 2 John 1 and 2 John 5. Some read this as a proper name as Young does and translate it so. Again as there is no simple straight counterpart in English for "quality" as an adjective, a word that matches the sentiment or meaning is needful. I choose "faithful" and Young as we see has "choice".

> The Elder to the choice Kyria, and to her children,
> whom I love in truth, and not I only, but also all
> those having known the truth,   *2 John 1 Young*

43

So that this,

> The Elder,
> To the elect lady and her children, whom I love in truth, and not only I, but also all those who have known the truth,   *2 John 1*

Then becomes,

> The Elder,
> To the faithful lady and her children, whom I love in truth, and not only I, but also all those who have known the truth,   *2 John 1 JM*

2 John 13
Same as 2 John 1 preceding I choose "faithful" and Young has picked "choice".

> Salute thee do the children of thy choice sister. Amen.
>   *2 John 13 Young*

So that,

> The children of your elect sister greet you. Amen.
>   *2 John 13*

Then becomes,

> The children of your faithful sister greet you. Amen.
>   *2 John 13 JM*

Revelation 17:14

The Young translation for *eklektos* is recognised as "choice" in various places and where he has used "chosen" or "elect" his notes as mentioned earlier introducing the New Testament clarify that this should be read as "choice one" so that this thorough man of learning in regards to every Hebrew and Greek word of the bible as per his analytical concordance saw *eklektos* in a similar light to what I am claiming. He translates *pistos* as "stedfast" here, but this word which means "faithful" or "trustworthy" is more commonly associated with *pisteuó* – to believe. I like "stedfast" for *eklektos* as an alternative quality rendering since "faithful" is being used alongside. Here is Young:

> . . . these with the Lamb shall make war, and the Lamb shall overcome them, because Lord of lords he is, and King of kings, and those with him are called, and choice, and stedfast.   *Revelation 17:14 Young*

So that,

> These will make war with the Lamb, and the Lamb will overcome them, for He is Lord of lords and King of kings; and those *who are* with Him *are* called, chosen, and faithful.   *Revelation 17:14*

Then becomes,

45

These will make war with the Lamb, and the Lamb
will overcome them, for He is Lord of lords and King
of kings; and those *who are* with Him *are* called,
stedfast, and faithful. *Revelation 17:14 JM*

5

SUNEKLEKTOS

There is only one place in the New Testament where this word is found and it is non existent in the Septuagint.

> She who is in Babylon, elect together with *you*, greets you; and *so does* Mark my son.   *1 Peter 5:13*

In the NKJV it is translated as "elect together with". Since *eklektos* is used for "elect" and "chosen" by that version and the preposition *sun* is about "with".

Sun

This preposition has a counterpart in English in that "syn-" or "sym-" is found in front of words. For example "sympathy" means suffering with.

But, as we saw in the preceding chapter *eklektos* is about quality and here at the end of his first letter Peter is continuing his thinking earlier expressed that just as his readers – the faithful sojourners of the dispersion of Pontus, Galatia, Cappadocia, Asia and Bithynia – were considered "**a faithful family, a royal priesthood, a holy nation, His own special people, that you may proclaim the praises of Him who**

called you out of darkness into His marvellous light" (1 Peter 2:9 JM), so also those in Babylon were likewise.

The literal Greek, word for word is "Salutes you she in Babylon *suneklekté* and Mark the son of me"

So that this is better read as:

> The church in Babylon, faithful with you, greets you; and so does Mark my son.   *1 Peter 5:13 JM*

6

GENEA

In this next chapter section about particular mistranslated Greek words, I wish to make a case for two different meanings of the one Greek word. This then affects the translation according to the context where the word is found. This is common in English where the words "chair" and "table" for example are easily understood as pieces of furniture, but in a different context can refer to something different like "The Chair of the committee suggested that was so." and "The table of contents is found in this book". The word *genea* is mostly recognised as to mean "a generation", but also found in its use within the Septuagint (LXX) it is seen not infrequently as "a family grouping", "a race", "kinsmen": i.e. a related grouping. This second meaning for *genea* has been taken into account by some translators of the New Testament, whilst others have occasionally made a note to that effect rather than adjust the translation. I am making a case for the second meaning in a set of places. I call them a set as the same subject is repeated elsewhere and I have re-arranged them to be seen together in "sets". Here is the quick list of examples of *genea* in the LXX as a related group:

Explicit examples of "Related Group" from *genea* in the LXX

Quick List

People of his time NIV	*genea*	Genesis 6:9
(their) **Birth** NIV	*geneón*	Genesis 25:13
(your) **kindred**	*genean*	Genesis 31:3
kindred	*genean*	Genesis 43:7
(their) **people**	*geneas*	Leviticus 20:18
Descendants NIV	*geneai*	Leviticus 23:43
Descendants NIV	*geneas*	Leviticus 25:30
Family – clan NIV	*genean*	Leviticus 25:41
Posterity	*geneais*	Numbers 9:10
kinsmen – **kindred** KJV	*genean*	Numbers 10:30
Descendants – **children** KJV	*geneai*	Numbers 13:22
Descendants – **children** KJV	*genean*	Numbers 13:28
Descendants NIV + NLT	*geneais*	Joshua 22:28
Descendants – **seed** KJV	*geneón*	Esther 9:28
(the) **Company** NIV	*genea*	Psalm 14:5
(Offspring) LXX only	*genea*	Proverbs 22:4
Descendants NIV + NLT	*genean*	Isaiah 53:8
Family – nation NIV	*geneas*	Jeremiah 8:3
Families – peoples NIV	*geneas*	Jeremiah 10:25

This list is expanded upon and then all the examples of *genea* in the LXX are given in the 2nd appendix.

So that when we read,

> Assuredly, I say to you, this generation will by no means pass away till all these things are fulfilled.
> *Matthew 24:34 – also Mark 13:30 and Luke 21:32*

I make a case for:

> This people [or this nation or this race] shall not pass away until these things take place.
> *Matthew 24:34 – also Mark 13:30 and Luke 21:32 JM*

When we read of Jesus speaking to the 12 apostles,

> O faithless and perverse generation, how long shall I
> be with you?
> > *Matthew 17:17 – also Mark 9:19 and Luke 9:41*

I believe a good paraphrase would then be read as:

> O faithless and perverse lot, how long shall I be
> with you?
> > *Matthew 17:17 – also Mark 9:19 and Luke 9:41 JM*

Or, where Peter says,

> But you *are* a chosen generation, a royal priesthood,
> a holy nation, His own special people . . .   *1 Peter 2:9*

It should instead be read, and here it is already well
translated differently by the NASB as:

> But you are a chosen race, a royal priesthood, a holy
> nation, a people for God's own possession . . .
> > *1 Peter 2:9 NASB*

Another is,

> For the sons of this world are more shrewd in their
> generation than the sons of light.   *Luke 16:8*

Which can be better understood as,

> For the sons of this age are more shrewd among their
> own kind than the sons of the light.   *Luke 16:8 JM*

In each of these places it is the group in view, the family of, or race, as opposed to a generation (of people) in a particular time length.

Now, this alternative rendering for *genea* is not altogether foreign as the NASB rendering of Peter above shows and this can be seen elsewhere with other translators. The NLT makes a note "Or this age, or this nation" for the Matthew 24:34 passage above and the same for Mark 13:30, but does not make it for the parallel passage in Luke 21:32. The NIV does make a note for all 3 places as "Or race". For 1 Peter 2:9 it is "a chosen people" in the NLT and the NIV whereas the NASB as mentioned already renders it as "a chosen race".

1. This people shall not pass away until all these things take place

Before we look at the word *genea* in detail, let's look at the exegetical evidence – the context of Scripture in regards to the same subject – that enables such a choice of an alternative rendering to be natural for what is being said in Matthew 24:34, Mark 13:30 and Luke 21:32 –

> THIS PEOPLE SHALL NOT PASS AWAY UNTIL
> ALL THESE THINGS TAKE PLACE.

Some would not taste of death till they saw the son of man coming in his kingdom

Now, in one of my KJV bibles there is a central page margin containing notes and cross references to other related passages. For the above passage of "**This generation shall not pass, till all these things be fulfilled**" (Matthew 24:34 KJV) the cross reference appears to a passage that allegedly says the same thing. Now, it would be understandable for the word *genea* to be translated in those 3 correlating prophetic passages as "generation" if the same thinking appears to be in view in an earlier saying of Jesus: if the subject is the same. Here is the passage cross-referred:

> For the Son of Man will come in the glory of His Father with His angels, and then He will reward each according to his works. Assuredly, I say to you, there are some standing here who shall not taste death till they see the Son of Man coming in His kingdom.
> *Matthew 16:27-28 – also Mark 9:1 and Luke 9:27*

If, some of the hearers of Jesus were not to die before Jesus coming in the glory of His Father with His angels then, that generation would also have indeed been the last one before Jesus' return. If that is what is meant here, then the cross reference is valid as is the meaning for "generation" from *genea*.

However in this alleged linked text in meaning, Jesus is careful in His emphatic statement "**Assuredly, I say to you...**" for in his ongoing words he limits what would be seen by those who would not die. Jesus limits it to: "**the Son of Man coming in his kingdom**". In the emphatic statement of what would be seen, no angels are mentioned or what he would do so it is not the same as what he mentioned in the preceding verse:

> For the Son of Man will come in the glory of His Father with His angels, and then He will reward each according to his works. *Matthew 16:27*

So that, when you see a limit to what is emphatic and can also recall that Jesus uses the phrase "**the kingdom of God has come upon you**" elsewhere, in a present emphasis, without any further future fulfilment understood, then no need here remains to believe that Jesus is talking about his full return to rule in the emphatic passage either. Here is an earlier mention of Jesus about the kingdom of God coming:

> If I cast out demons by the Spirit of God, surely the kingdom of God has come upon you. *Matthew 12:28*

Here, Jesus uses the phrase "**the kingdom of God has come upon you**" about something in the present lifetime of his hearers. So that we see in his already established use of language Jesus saying "**the kingdom of God has come**" can be just about a manifestation of God's power in the present.

Jesus said some of his hearers would actually see something before they died. But the point is made that Jesus said what they would see: that is, he as – the Son of Man – "**coming in his kingdom**". Since we now know that the kingdom having come is clearly read as relevant in the present in the example of the power of God demonstrated in the casting out demons, when you then read the immediately following verses about the transfiguration, you get the picture that this is what Jesus meant would be seen before some of the disciples died. I believe this was understood by all the synoptic gospel writers and is shown us by their very placing of that emphatic statement before the transfiguration. What he was referring to is thus fully revealed. Matthew 16:28, Mark 9:1 and Luke 9:27 with the statement are immediately followed respectively by the transfiguration in Matthew 17:1-13, Mark 9:2-13 and Luke 9:28-36. The transfiguration is a full visual demonstration of the Son of Man coming in his kingdom: no more. This happened in full view of Peter, James and John who thereby saw Jesus as the Son of Man come in His kingdom before they died. In the same manner as Jesus used that phrase to refer to casting out demons as a demonstration of the kingdom of God as having come.

It is helpful to remember when the chapter divisions were put into the bible in the 13th century and the verses in the 16th that these aids to locating passages have proved very useful. But, by the act of dividing connected passages, these very divisions distract from the recognition of context: that is to say – always – the transfiguration account is preceded by the statement that some standing there would not taste death till they had seen the Son of Man coming in his kingdom. It is not incidental thereby that it is not Jesus' return in view, but the manifestation of God's power and glory at the transfiguration.

So the mention that some of Jesus' hearers would not taste death till they had seen the Son of Man coming in his kingdom, since it is not a reference to Jesus' 2nd coming itself, does not correlate with an understanding that *genea* means "generation" in our initial 3 passages. This means there should be no cross reference between these unrelated passages.

There is further proof that the disciples were not expecting Jesus' return in their lifetime and this is given us in that at least 2 knew that one of them would die whilst old. If you know you're going to die an old man, then you know you're not going to see Jesus' return when that is a time when you expect to live on forever.

Disciples not expecting Jesus' return in their lifetime
John and Peter both knew – because of what Jesus said to them – that Peter was going to die whilst old and in a manner not preferred. This meant they did not expect Jesus to return before that event.

To Simon Peter Jesus said:

> . . . Simon . . . when you were younger, you girded yourself and walked where you wished; but when

> you are old, you will stretch out your hands, and
> another will gird you and carry *you* where you do
> not wish.   *John 21:15-18*

John goes on to explain:

> This He spoke, signifying by what death he would
> glorify God . . .   *John 21:19*

Clearly Jesus said to Peter "**when you are old**" so that
we know from this the disciples did not expect Jesus'
return in their lifetime.

Other pointers exegetically to the fact that the
people of Israel are in view as to remain till the end
are found in the Old Testament.

Definite prophecies of Israel remaining till the end
In Jeremiah we read:

> Thus says the LORD, who gives the sun for a light by
> day, *and* the ordinances of the moon and the stars
> for a light by night, who disturbs the sea, and its
> waves roar (The LORD of hosts *is* His name): "If those
> ordinances depart from before Me, says the LORD,
> then the seed of Israel shall also cease from being a
> nation before Me forever."   *Jeremiah 31:35-36*

Are the sun and moon still giving light?
     Yes.
     Is Israel, as a people and nation still around?

Yes.

Did Matthew 24, Mark 13 and Luke 21 mention the sun and the moon not giving light?

Did Jesus mention these "ordinances" would be for signs?

Yes.

Where?

> . . . after the tribulation . . . the sun will be darkened, and the moon will not give its light . . .
>
> *Matthew 24:29 & Mark 13:24*

> And there will be signs in the sun, in the moon, and in the stars . . . *Luke 21:25*

So here we have a positive exegetical sign ☺ [for the pun] that Jesus meant Israel as "a race", "a people", when he used the word *genea* in the 3 passages I began with.

This is further attested to in Daniel:

> Seventy weeks are determined for your people and for your holy city, to finish the transgression, to make an end of sins, to make reconciliation for iniquity, to bring in everlasting righteousness, to seal up vision and prophecy, and to anoint the Most Holy.
>
> *Daniel 9:24*

Now, the word for "**weeks**" here is literally a "sevens" from the Hebrew word *shabua*. It is translated literally in Ezekiel 45:21 as such "**you shall observe the Passover, a feast of seven days**": What this tells us is that to Daniel was said, "**Seventy sevens are determined *for your people* . . . to seal up vision and prophecy . . .**" (emphasis mine). It tells us Daniel's people would remain till the end.

Who are Daniel's people?

The Jews, Israel.

The seventy sevens and the ending of prophecy are not complete: Israel will be here till these things have taken place. (For further reading into the meaning of the "seventy sevens" I recommend my article *A possible understanding for the year of the Lord's return* presently available to read at www.jarom.net)

Thus the Jeremiah and Daniel passages are parallel in meaning to our 3 in question and exegetically it makes full and good sense to render *genea* there as "race" or "people" since all these tell us prophecy is not done before the demise of Israel as a people.

I think thereby we can be emphatic that context provides for us that Israel as a people is in view and not a generation when we see *genea* in Matthew 24:34. Mark 13:30 and Luke 21:32

> This people shall not pass away until all these things take place.
> *Matthew 24:34. Mark 13:30 and Luke 21:32 JM*

2. O faithless and perverse lot, how long shall I be with you?

You unbelieving and perverse group of guys
I began with 3 parallel passages that needed change and trust I have given enough to persuade you of this. I then mentioned this set of 3:

> O faithless and perverse generation, how long shall I be with you?
>> *Matthew 17:17- also Mark 9:19 and Luke 9:41*

Where a good paraphrase would then be read as:

> O faithless and perverse lot, how long shall I be with you?
>> *Matthew 17:17- also Mark 9:19 and Luke 9:41 JM*

The scene is set for us in that Jesus is not present, but only the disciples and a father comes to them with his son requesting that they cast out a demon afflicting the boy. Some time passes by and when Jesus returns to the scene with Peter, James and John – all having descended from the mount where the transfiguration occurred (see Matthew 17:1-18 or the parallel passages) – the father then informs Jesus that the disciples were asked to cast out this demon, but they were not able. This is when Jesus then says:

> O faithless and perverse *GENEA*, how long shall I be with you? How long shall I bear with you? Bring him here to Me.
>> *Matthew 17:17*

Then Jesus rebukes the demon and the child was cured. Then privately the disciples came to Jesus and asked why they could not do it. Jesus' immediate words were,

> Because of your unbelief . . .   *Matthew 17:20*

Whose unbelief? Answer: The unbelief of the disciples that tried to cast the demon out.

Was the generation of people at that time in view? Answer: No.

So here, Jesus' use of *genea* is a reference to the disciples as a related group: the unbelieving ones Jesus was grieved about. This qualifies this set of 3 parallel passages to then be translated as:

> O faithless and perverse group of guys, how long shall I be with you?
> *Matthew 17:17- Mark 9:19 – Luke 9:41 JM*

Alternative renderings are "followers", "guys", and so on. As already mentioned, my immediate favourite would serve a paraphrase well:

> O faithless and perverse lot, how long shall I be with you?
> *Matthew 17:17 – also Mark 9:19 and Luke 9:41 JM*

Here is the NLT:

> Jesus said to them, 'You faithless people! How long must I be with you? How long must I put up with you? Bring the boy to me.' *Mark 9:19 NLT*

For the sons of this age are more shrewd among their own kind

I started with mentioning 2 sets of passages and then 2 single verses.

Since there are 2 separate meanings for *genea* as demonstrated above and in full within the references and quotes from the Septuagint in the 2nd Appendix, it remains up to the context and the other references to the same topic to reveal what is meant. I believe I have shown this in regards to Israel as a people being in view with Jesus saying "this *genea* shall not pass away until these things take place" and with the disciples as a group being declared unbelieving.

So that knowing there are these two different meanings for *genea* when we read,

> For the sons of this world are more shrewd in their generation than the sons of light. *Luke 16:8*

You can understand how I would translate this as,

> For the sons of this age are more shrewd among their own kind than the sons of the light. *Luke 16:8 JM*

However I feel I cannot be so emphatic in translating *genea* this way when we read "this generation seeks after a sign" and think this can mean either the people of Israel, the Jews or the generation at the time.

This generation seek after a sign

The Jews seek after a sign
Here is a passage which by the context can be understood either way. Jesus said,

> An evil and adulterous generation seeks after a sign...
> *Matthew 12:39 also 16:4, Mark 8:12 and Luke 11:29*

Now, this can be meant either as written: "generation" or a "race", a "grouping". Here is what gives us the latter. Paul wrote:

> For Jews request a sign, and Greeks seek after wisdom... *1 Corinthians 1:22*

Here we see Paul telling us that the Jews as a people, as a race, are those who seek after a sign. So that exegetically it is sound to translate *genea* in Matthew 12:39 as "**An evil and adulterous race/people seeks after a sign**" but I do not think this can be forced, as the generation of people at the time are well addressed also in various places as being evil, unfaithful and unfit for the kingdom. I would not use it for this passage because in the same breath Jesus goes on to say - only a few verses later:

The men of Nineveh will rise up in the judgment with this generation [*genea*] and condemn it, because they repented at the preaching of Jonah; and indeed a greater than Jonah *is* here. The queen of the South will rise up in the judgment with this generation [*genea*] and condemn it, for she came from the ends of the earth to hear the wisdom of Solomon; and indeed a greater than Solomon *is* here.   *Matthew 12:41-42*

Which goes with,

> . . . the last *state* of that man is worse than the first. So shall it also be with this wicked generation.
>   *Matthew 12:45*

And also goes with what Jesus expressed earlier speaking of groups of people in that generation,

> Woe to you, Chorazin! Woe to you, Bethsaida! For if the mighty works which were done in you had been done in Tyre and Sidon, they would have repented long ago in sackcloth and ashes.   *Matthew 11:21*

So that although Paul clearly refers to the Jews seeking after a sign as a people, Jesus goes on to give examples of his preaching and his wisdom and the miracles he did in that time and that if they had been done in an earlier generation they would have been recognised.

This then makes the following examples of *genea* good translations as "generation"

Matthew 11:16	*tén genean tautén*	to what shall I liken this generation?
Matthew 12:41	*tés geneas tautés*	rise in the judgment with this generation
Matthew 12:42	*tés geneas tautés*	queen of the South will rise up... in the judgment with this generation
Matthew 12:45	*té genea tauté*	the last *state* of that man is worse than the first... So shall it also be with this wicked generation
Matthew 23:36	*tén genean tautén*	I say to you, all these things... will come upon this generation.
Mark 8:38	*té genea tauté*	whoever is ashamed of Me and My words... in this adulterous and sinful generation
Luke 1:50	*eis geneas geneón*	And His mercy *is* on those who fear Him... From generation to generation.
Luke 7:31	*tés geneas tautés*	what then shall I liken the men of this generation
Luke 11:29	*hé genea hauté*	This is an evil generation. It seeks a sign
Luke 11:30	*té genea tauté*	so also the Son of Man will be to this generation
Luke 11:31	*tés geneas tautés*	will rise up in the judgment with the men of this generation and condemn them

Luke 11:32	*tés geneas tautés*	in the judgment with this generation and condemn it
Luke 11:50	*tés geneas tautés*	from the foundation of the world may be required of this generation
Luke 11:51	*tés geneas tautés*	I say to you, it shall be required of this generation.
Luke 17:25	*tés geneas tautés*	many things and be rejected by this generation
Acts 2:40	*tés geneas*	Be saved from this perverse generation
Hebrews 3:10	*té genea ekeiné*	*Therefore I was angry with that generation*

All these refer to "generation" in context and are good translations.

Other mentions that are open to discussion are as follows:

| Acts 8:33 | *tén de genean autou* | *In His humiliation His justice was taken away, and who will declare His* **generation**? *For His life is taken from the earth* "He was humiliated and received no justice. Who can speak of his **descendants**? For his life was taken from the earth" Acts 8:33 NLT |
| Acts 13:36 | *idia genea* | after he had served his own **generation** by the will of God |

66

Philippians 2:15   *geneas skolias*   that you may become
blameless and harmless,
children of God without
fault in the midst of a
crooked and perverse
generation, among
whom you shine as
lights in the world
"in a world full of
crooked and perverse
people." Philippians
2:15 NLT

To recap the passages to reconsider are:
Literal:

> This people shall not pass away until all these things
> take place.
> > *Matthew 24:34. Mark 13:30 and Luke 21:32 JM*

As a paraphrase:

> O faithless and perverse group of guys, how long
> shall I be with you?
> > *Matthew 17:17- Mark 9:19 – Luke 9:41 JM*

As literal,

> But you are a chosen race, a royal priesthood, a holy
> nation, a people for God's own possession . . .
> > *1 Peter 2:9 NASB*

And,

For the sons of this age are more shrewd among their own kind than the sons of the light.

Luke 16:8 JM

7

TASSÓ – ACTS 13:48

The word I wish to share in this chapter within the section about words that have been mistranslated is the verb *tassó*. This has been primarily translated as "to appoint" to the detriment of good understanding and in particular in regards to a passage used as a "proof text" to support a 5th century doctrine that God decides everything in regards to salvation. Namely Acts 13:48,

> Now when the Gentiles heard this, they were glad and glorified the word of the Lord. And as many as had been appointed to eternal life believed.   *Acts 13:48*

If this were a true and valid translation then you can see how this lends itself to a "proof text" use in support of any dogma that God chooses who is saved.

Acts 13:48
Acts 13:48 is here explained in context of Paul's use of the same verb tense elsewhere and Luke's practise of using *hosoi* – "as many as" – to show God is not viewed in this passage as the one "appointing".

> . . . as many as had been appointed to eternal life
> believed. *Acts 13:48*

As it stands this passage really reads like a done deal doesn't it?

God, since who else could be "appointing" in such matters, is here.

God then, is read – as allocating – eternal life (to whom He will) as a result of which these are the ones seen to believe. It looks that way, doesn't it?

Those appointed to eternal life – they believed?

Yes?

Well, not quite.

You see, this is only possible if the verb in question is accurately translated as "appointed" or "ordained" (as per the KJV). For it is only in those words being used – "appointed" or "ordained" – that the implication is given that someone else other than the believer is involved.

So, how else is the Greek verb *tassó* translated in the New Testament?

Well, before we look at that, let's re-arrange the words to the way they appear in the Greek.

> *kai episteusan hosoi ésan tetagmenoi eis zóén aiónion*
>
> and (they) believed as many as (they) were TASSÓ into life eternal
>
> N.B. Emphasis Mine for all the mentions of the verbs in or out of quotes below.

Let's highlight each section:

> "*kai episteusan*" – and they believed
>
> "*hosoi ésan tetagmenoi*" – as many as they were TASSÓ
>
> "*eis zóén aiónion*" – to life eternal

Further, let's make clear about "They were" – The verb "to be" in Greek is as follows in the Imperfect tense (English Past Continuous):

Greek	English
Émén	I was
és or éstha	you were
én	he, she, it was
émen or émetha	we were
éte	you were
ésan	they were

So, in the same order, literally from the Greek, we have:

> And they believed, as many as they were *TASSÓ* into life eternal   *Acts 13:48*

Remember "They were" is a full and accurate translation of *ésan* apart and distinct from *TASSÓ* and its tense in the sentence.

So, let's look at what else *TASSÓ* has been translated into.

71

1 Corinthians 16:15 – *etaxan*

> they have ADDICTED themselves to the ministry of the
> saints   *KJV*

> they have DEVOTED themselves...   *NKJV*

> to the ministration to the saints they did SET
> themselves   *Young*

This would make Acts 13:48 read:

> And they believed, as many as they were ADDICTED
> into life eternal

> And they believed, as many as they were DEVOTED into
> life eternal

> And they believed, as many as they were SET into life
> eternal

Note how God now is not implied in the action of
the verb by the very change in the verb translation
itself.

Acts 15:2 – *etaxan*

> They DETERMINED that Paul and Barnabas
> *KJV, NKJV*

they ARRANGED for Paul and Barnabas   *Young*

This would make Acts 13:48 read:

> And they believed, as many as THEY were DETERMINED into life eternal

> And they believed, as many as THEY were ARRANGED into life eternal

Note here how God could be implied, but so can the believers alone as doing the action of the verb, especially if "They" is emphasised.

Luke 7:8 – *tassomenos*

> I also am a man SET under authority   *KJV*

> I also am a man PLACED under authority
> *NKJV & Young*

This would make Acts 13:48 read

> And they believed, as many as they were SET into life eternal

> And they believed, as many as they were PLACED into life eternal

So, we can see the following words are also used for *TASSÓ*

addicted, devoted, set, determined, arranged, placed

The verb *TASSÓ* is also used extensively in the Septuagint (LXX) – The Greek version of the Old Testament Jesus and the apostles quoted. For every place in the LXX see appendix 3. Also at the end of the appendix is the list of all the other Greek verbs used in the New Testament for the words "ordain" and "appoint" (KJV).

In Ezekiel 40:4 for example – remember this is the English translation of the Hebrew text, not of the LXX and shows the verb from which *tassó* in the LXX has been used - we read

> FIX your mind on everything I show you
> *Ezekiel 40:4*

Margin: Lit. SET your heart

Translated as the Verb *tassó* in the LXX and conjugated as *taxon*

In Ezekiel 44:5 we read

> And the LORD said to me, 'Son of man, MARK WELL, see with your eyes and hear with your ears, all that I say to you'　　*Ezekiel 44:5*

Margin: Lit. SET your heart.

Translated as the Verb *tassó* in the LXX and conjugated as *taxon*

In Haggai 1:5 we read

> Now therefore, thus says the LORD of hosts: 'CONSIDER your ways!' *Haggai 1:5*

> SET your heart to your ways *Young*

Translated as the verb *tassó* in the LXX and conjugated as *taxate*

Appoint or Ordain

We've now seen what else *TASSÓ* can mean. And we've seen in numerous places it is used as a personal action; not just someone else's action. But, before we move on, let's go back to the N.T. where it is translated **"appoint"** or **"ordain"** and note that in every other instance of these, it is clear who is appointing.

Matthew 28:16 – *etaxato*

> To the mountain which Jesus had appointed for them *Matthew 28:16*

Acts 22:10 – tetaktai

> You will be told all things which are appointed for you to do *Acts 22:10*

Acts 28:23 – *taxamenoi*

So when they had appointed him a day   *Acts 28:23*

Romans 13:1 – *tetagmenai*

The authorities that exist are appointed by God
Romans 13:1

The powers that be are ordained of God
Romans 13:1 KJV

There is no room for movement in any of these:

It is JESUS who appointed the mountain as the place (Matthew 28:16); Are appointed FOR THEE (Acts 22:10); Had appointed HIM (Acts 28:23); Are ordained OF GOD (Romans 13:1). It is clear who is appointing in all mentions: Unlike Acts 13:48 where "THEY were determined" or "THEY were appointed".

Now, Robert Young in his concordance liberally refers to *tassó* as "To arrange"

ADDICT – to arrange, set oneself
APPOINT – to arrange, set in order
DETERMINE – to arrange
ORDAIN – to arrange, set in array
SET – to arrange, set in array

The flavour can be even more visible when comparing with *diatassó*, *epitassó*, *suntassó*, *protassomai* and *prostassó*

In the conjugation of *tassó* seen above in the LXX from Ezekiel 40:4 and 44:5 we see *tassó* conjugated as *taxon*. It is not hard then with ARRANGE as the core meaning to see where our English word "taxonomy" comes from: The word for the classification of species. It is about the "arrangement", the "order" of things.

It is not about a specific determination, but an arrangement. So even with the verb "to appoint" it is possible with "arrange" in mind to understand an order and arrangement, not a specific (allocation). For example in Romans 13:1 we read

> Let every soul be subject to the governing authorities. For there is no authority except from God, and the authorities that exist are appointed by God.
>
> *Romans 13:1*

We read, "**The authorities that exist are appointed by God**": The authorities are arranged, they are set in order by God. By the word's root use therefore it is not saying the particular individual is in power by God, but instead Paul's emphasis by that word is that the office of ruler or judge is in place by God: It is the office of such authority in view; not the particular person in place as an authority in these arrangements.

Acts 13:48
If we go back to Acts 13:48, what do we find?

No particular individuals specified by the core "arrangement" meaning of *TASSÓ*. By that use of the verb God ceases to be implied as doing the action. Instead, the individuals are left in doing the action. They are seen having arranged their hearts to eternal life: It is THEY who WERE determined or set (arranged) in their hearts to believe: and because of that they did. And this can also be seen from the context.

The context points to the attitude of heart present:

It is about the new believers in Act 13:48 IN CONTRAST TO the unbelievers who opposed Paul in Acts 13:45-46. What opposition?

> But when the Jews saw the multitudes, they were filled with envy; and contradicting and blaspheming, they opposed the things spoken by Paul . . .
>
> *Acts 13:45*

The unbelieving Jews were in opposition.

Of these Paul then says:

> It was necessary that the word of God should be spoken to you first; but since YOU reject it, and JUDGE YOURSELVES UNWORTHY of everlasting life, behold we turn to the Gentiles. *Acts 13:46*

We read then, THEY – the unbelieving Jews – judged themselves "unworthy of everlasting life": *aióniou dzóés*

– life eternal/everlasting (Acts 13:46). And, using the same words in Acts 13:48 – *dzóén aiónion* – we see a link between these 2 verses.

So that "THEY were determined" or "THEY were set" makes good sense for *TASSÓ* in Acts 13:48.

But why did Luke write this at all?

We have a clue by his regular practise of using *hosoi* – as many as. It is to limit the "all" which Luke previously mentions so the reader is not to think everyone is involved in becoming believers. Luke uses *hosoi* – as many as – like this in the Greek of Acts 5:36, Acts 5:37 and Acts 10:45. It was his common practise - To limit the ALL suggested beforehand.

Acts 5:36

> For some time ago Theudas rose up, claiming to be somebody. A number of men, about four hundred, joined him. He was slain, and all who obeyed him were scattered and came to nothing.   *Acts 5:36*

This translation does not show the Greek which compares with Acts 13:48, so here is the Greek:

Hos – anérethé – kai – pantes – hosoi – epeithonto – autó – dieluthésan – kai – egenonto – eis – ouden

Who – was put to death – and – all – as many as – were persuaded – by him – were dispersed – and – came – to – nothing

79

"And all, as many as were persuaded" Luke uses "all" followed by "as many as" to limit all's extent.

Acts 5:37

> After this man, Judas of Galilee rose up in the days of the census, and drew away many people after him. He also perished, and all who obeyed him were dispersed. *Acts 5:37*

This translation also does not show the Greek "comparison" I wish to show, here it is in this case:

> *Kakeinos – apóleto – kai – pantes – hosoi – epeithonto – autó – dieskorpisthésan*
>
> And he – perished – and – all – as many as – were persuaded – by him – were scattered abroad

This is a repeat identical in practise to the previous verse with "as many as" immediately following "all".

Acts 10:45

> And those of the circumcision who believed were astonished, as many as came with Peter . . .
> *Acts 10:45*

Here, the word all is not mentioned, nor is it in the Greek, but Luke's use of "as many as" is clear. He mentions Jewish believers – that is believers in Jesus that were among the Jews. But, not all those who are believers, only those who came with Peter are clarified. This is Luke's common use of *hosoi* – "as many as" to limit and remove a possible implication that the preceding words meant everyone he just mentioned.

So that in Acts 13 since Luke had said "THE WHOLE CITY" came to hear (13:44) – THE GENTILES heard (13:48a) AND they believed (13:48b – remember the order in the Greek), Luke NOT wanting the idea read that ALL believed, he adds "as many as" they were determined (13:48c). Luke's important point is that there were many new believers: "And they believed" But not all who came to hear did so.

Now, it is EXPLICIT that *ésan* = they were

So that "THEY were determined" Luke just adds the section to reduce the number of new believers in the readers mind.

Conclusion

The whole city came together to hear (V.44)

And they believed (V.48a)

As many as THEY were determined to life everlasting (V.48b)

Devoted, set, arranged (in their hearts)

And the Gentiles hearing rejoiced, and glorified the word of the Lord and they believed as many as they were determined to life eternal.   *Acts 13:48 JM*

81

UN-TRANSLATED WORDS

8

THREE MEASURES OF MEAL

Matthew 13:33 – Luke 13:20-21

Here is an example of a mistranslation due to a basic and simple word *tria* = "three" not being translated. This parable depends on the word "three" to be understood and without it prevents this parable to be of any use at all.

The translator, having no understanding of what was meant in the text and for the sake of being seen to produce a version in "modern" English does not translate this word but instead replaces it with an alternative which removes any possibility of any one understanding the parable.

Let me make this plain, Jesus' parable of the 3 (1+1+1) measures of meal makes no sense whatsoever as one "large amount" NIV. The same is true of the Good News Translation "with a bushel of flour" or *The message* "the dough for dozens of loaves of barley bread" in Matthew or "enough dough for three loaves of bread" as in Luke [awful!] and others. Though in the NIV a note is added in both places of Matthew 13:33 and Luke 13:21 to show Jesus mentions "three", the focus of the note is on the quantity and not the actual number "three". Here is the note: "Greek *three satas* (probably about 3/5 bushel or 22 litres)": thus revealing the purpose of the word "three" is not understood.

The deal here is the bible is not like other books. It is the inspired word of God. And the less accurate you are with the translation the more you lose (often) from the meaning. There is a place for paraphrase and I fully approve of them. But to make claim of a translation to accuracy *when* it is clearly more a paraphrase than a translation does not help with sound doctrine or beneficial teaching. This parable is a good example of that and is a pointer to place the NIV in a category of a mistranslated paraphrase version here.

> The kingdom of heaven is like yeast that a woman took and mixed into a large amount of flour until it worked all through the dough.   *Matthew 13:33 NIV*

Here is the NKJV translation.

> The kingdom of heaven is like leaven, which a woman took and hid in three measures of meal till it was all leavened.   *Matthew 13:33 NKJV*

Now, I need to compliment the NIV for bringing up to date the language with terms such as "yeast" instead of "leaven" as well as "flour" and "dough" instead of "meal" and "leavened". Equally "mixed into" is more understandable than "hid in". But the very purpose of the parable is lost by having "a large amount" when "three measures" is at the heart of the thinking behind the parable. Of course it does not help translators when they rely on current dogma, teaching and belief about a passage rather than the correct grammar and actual inspired words involved in Greek. Perhaps, if the meaning of this story by Jesus was widely spread, the Greek word *treis*, (*tria*) for "three" would never have been removed in the "translation" of this passage.

Understanding

So, let's explain the importance of the 3 in this passage.

To begin let's note that Jesus is quoted as teaching this alongside another parable which is written before the 3 measures of meal parable.

> The kingdom of heaven is like a mustard seed, which a man took and sowed in his field, which indeed is the least of all the seeds; but when it is grown it is greater than the herbs and becomes a tree, so that the birds of the air come and nest in its branches.   *Matthew 13:31-32*

In Luke 13:18-21 and Matthew 13:31-33 we find both these parables together. In Mark 4:30-32 we find the mustard seed into a tree parable on its own and Mark does not contain the other parable. But where the 3 measures of meal parable is, the other is there preceding it.

Jesus here tells 2 separate stories in regards to the kingdom of heaven and its relationship with a person.

These are together because 2 separate emphases are told us in how kingdom life comes about in the life of the individual:

The first involves a hidden and natural progressive growth which develops without conscious effort into a full blown fruitful life in the kingdom of God. The mustard seed becomes a full grown tree.

The second parable – the one to uncover and explain – involves the 3 separate amounts of meal or flour to be handled and speaks of the personal conscious effort and responsibility of the individual to work things through.

In Jesus' day and for many centuries later, let alone today in remote or less developed world economic societies, the 2nd parable makes easier sense. The daily need and practise to knead dough in the making of bread or other flour based food is a world apart from many lives today. A trip to the supermarket, the local bakery or even a daily delivery by your milkman (UK) removes the experience and appreciation of what is involved in making bread.

What is involved?

If you have a large amount of dough to prepare, then it needs separating into workable batches. This is because if you are alone and indeed both parables talk about a single person, then you need to set aside what is not physically possible to deal with on your own until the first batch is fully prepared. There is a lot of effort and concentration in kneading a batch of dough. The yeast that has been added to the ready mix of flour and water needs to be "worked in" very thoroughly. This is done by kneading: the work of massaging and thoroughly mixing the ingredients together. And here is the point of having 3 batches mentioned. You cannot move on to the 2nd batch until you have fully finished handling and mixing thoroughly the 1st batch. And you cannot go on to handle the 3rd batch until you have thoroughly mixed the 2nd. The idea then is of handling what is manageable one at a time. If only 2 batches had been mentioned, in practise you can get away with mixing them all at once together, it just takes a little longer. But in having 3 batches you cannot. There really is too much to handle at once. There is no need to mention more than 3 because the multitude is not the issue, but the very need to handle a manageable batch of dough to permeate with yeast at any one time. This is the point of the parable.

In our lives there are issues of sin one may be struggling with, or an area of character that is particularly challenging, or an area of opportunity the Lord has placed before us. The deal is some of these things require our full and undivided conscious attention before one can move on to the next issue in hand. So, the need is to recognise what is the most important thing the Lord sees as required for us to concentrate on at this time. The enemy would want to discourage us by pointing to other things that are needful also. But the Lord expects and encourages us to deal with what we can handle one at a time. To leave the rest aside whilst the one is thoroughly mixed into the kingdom life pattern required.

Christians are encouraged to be Overcomers

Jesus said,

> To him who overcomes I will give . . .
> *Revelation 2:7, 17, (see also 2:11, 26; 3:5, 12, 21)*

But also, not to be overly troubled,

> For My yoke is easy and My burden is light.
> *Matthew 11:30*

The reason the 2 parables are together is that a personal balance is to be gained. The work of the kingdom involves letting God patiently work in and through us his will, purposes and transformation as well as knowing the individual things we are faced with handling and dealing with ourselves.

Another good use of the three measure of meal parable is to combine it with Jesus' mention of needing to be single of eye.

> The lamp of the body is the eye. If therefore your eye
> is good, your whole body will be full of light
> *Matthew 6:22*

Yes, I did say "single". Here it is in the Authorised Version (KJV).

> The light of the body is the eye. If therefore thine eye be single, thy whole body shall be full of light.
>
> *Matthew 6:22 KJV*

The Greek word for "good" is *agathos*. Here the Greek word in the sentence is *haploos*, found here in its declension *haplous*. This word is only found twice in the New Testament; the other text which contains it is the parallel passage in Luke 11:34. The word is related to *haplotés* and *haplós* which mean "simplicity", "sincerity", "purity" and the latter, "simply", "sincerely". I suppose not dissimilarly to *apistos* the Greek word for "unbelieving", "unfaithful" which is in contrast to *pistos* for "believing", "faithful", so *haploos* can be contrasted to *plousios* which means "rich", "abounding in", "full" (could *plousios* be a source of the word "plus"?).

So, *haploos* in contrast is to be "single", "alone" or clearly seeing only one thing – in that sense – to be with only one "simple" view of what one sees: Hence the fact of its translation as "**single**" of eye in the KJV. If you combine this idea of being single minded with the 3 measures of meal parable where the person is to concentrate on one thing at a time, then it is useful in teaching to live a moment at a time with all one's mind and heart and strength involved in the moment. To build the kingdom one moment and one task at a time fully concentrating on that: with excellence in the little things, in the moment, thus producing over time a beautiful and well crafted whole.

So, what do you think? Is the following paraphrase close in giving the meaning of our passage?

> Another story. "God's kingdom is like yeast that a woman works into the dough for dozens of loaves of barley bread – and waits while the dough rises."
>
> *Matthew 13:33 The message*

It is important then for translators of any language – and this is translation 101 – to understand what is being said before attempting to put this to another set of words in a different language.

> The kingdom of heaven is like yeast that a woman took and mixed into three measures of flour until it was all worked through the dough.
>
> *Matthew 13:33 JM*

9

1 CORINTHIANS 11:3

In this un-translated word category I have placed 1 Corinthians 11:3 mainly because the accurate meaning of a word has not been translated in several important versions. The contents of this chapter and that of the later one on 1 Timothy 2:12 are borrowed from my book *Leadership is male?* – A work on the topic of women in leadership from a previous advocate of male leadership – as I was – explaining a way through the passages without side-tracking them and perhaps one of the few books on the subject [the only?] that makes the central argument that deception is the main deal in Paul's writing on this subject. I believe any book not explaining deception misses completely what Paul was saying. In the process of study and research for the book I discovered that 2 of the passages affecting the subject were mistranslated: 1 Corinthians 11:3 in a few versions and 1 Timothy 2:12 in most. I have adapted the contents of those chapters to the purposes of this book. Also due to the length of the word studies these have been placed as appendices 4 and 5.

The late John Wimber, founding leader of the Vineyard Christian Fellowships was interviewed in the *European Christian Bookstore Journal* (August 1993 issue Page 35). On the topic of women in leadership he made brief mention that in his understanding women are prohibited in scripture from involvement in the government of the church; it is a gender issue. He said that prohibition comes primarily from three texts in the New Testament. This topic was only briefly covered and there was no mention as to which texts were involved.

As a reader familiar with the issue "the three" passages immediately came to my mind: those contained in 1 Corinthians 11, 1 Corinthians 14 and 1 Timothy 2. John Stott in his book *Issues Facing Christians Today* discusses this topic. For him the main passage which prohibits women from governing in the church is that of 1 Corinthians 11:3; it is as far as I could see his "final hurdle". Personally, as mentioned in my book Preface I "stood beside" David Pawson and his book *Leadership Is Male* for quite a while and would have certainly approved of John Wimber's thinking; but, following further research and a number of discoveries in the Bible texts relevant to the issue, I am now totally committed to a full role for women in leadership.

Allow me then to address the first text mentioned, that of 1 Corinthians 11: as far as the issue is concerned it primarily deals with Verse 3 and is about the headship of man over woman:

> . . . the head of every man is Christ; the head of woman *is* man; and the head of Christ *is* God.
>
> *1 Corinthians 11:3*

The significant portion is "the head of the woman is man" In the Greek text we find, *kephalé-de gunaikos ho anér* That is, "but/and head of woman/wife the man/husband". Like the French "femme", in Greek there is only one word for "wife" and "woman", that of *guné*. Equally for "man" and "husband" there is only one word, *anér*. It is from this word that we get the English "android": a robot that looks like a man: like "Data" the brilliantly played android by Brent Spiner of *Star trek – The Next Generation.*

So that in order to know which word to translate into the English version, often the context will help clarify, whether a wife and husband is being mentioned as opposed to a woman and a man.

There is also another word for "man" that of *anthrópos*. It is from this word that we get the English "anthropology": the study of peoples. What is the difference between *anér* and *anthrópos*? You may ask. In my research, I have looked at every place where *anér* is to be found in the New Testament in whatever form it is found: see appendix 4 for *anér* and appendix 5 for *anthrópos*. By a different "form" I am referring to whether it was in the singular or plural and in every declension for that word. A declension is an adaptation of a word so it looks different: like *gunaikos* and *guné* as already to be observed above. These are an essential part of the New Testament Greek language.

Declensions in Greek
In English, if I said "a man speaks to an angel." it

would mean something different to "an angel speaks to a man". This is because the order in the sentence in which the words appear are different, but not the way the words themselves appear. No word has changed form. The meaning has changed only by the different arrangement. In Greek the order of the words in the sentence is not as important as the relationship between the words of a sentence. This interaction is shown by changing the endings of words thus revealing the relationship. This change in the endings and forms of a word is known as a declension.

Anér is the word as it is found when it is the subject of a verb – the nominative case. This is the form presented and first seen in lists of words, lexicons and dictionaries. The same word *anér* changes into the form *andra* when it is the direct object/recipient of the action of a verb – the accusative case, *andros* in the genitive (hence the link with "android"), and so on.

Anér and Anthrópos

So, having looked at *anér* in all its forms and comparing it with the use of *anthrópos*, in particular when both are translated in English as "man", a clear picture arises.

Anér

Strong's lexicon asserts "a man (properly as an individual male)" – (Strong's Exhaustive Concordance of the Bible including Dictionary of the Greek Testament by James Strong of Abingdon, Nashville: Page 12 of lexicon).

I agree. My research shows *anér* is used to express "a particular man" whilst *anthrópos* has the emphasis of "any man, a type of person, someone, etc".

> *Anér* = a (particular) man or, a husband
> *Anthrópos* = a man (any), a person, someone

Anthrópos is therefore the word Jesus uses when he calls himself "the Son of Man" because he is not the son of a particular man, but of mankind. This distinction shows up well in the plural since *anér* will then be used for a particular group of male persons whilst *anthrópos* has the emphasis on "peoples" including men and women.

A good example
Both words in the same verse in John's gospel can be seen when the feeding of the 5,000 is mentioned:

> Then Jesus said, 'Make the people [*anthrópous*] sit down.' Now there was much grass in the place. So the men [*Andres*] sat down, in number about five thousand. *John 6:10*

As soon as the men had been counted in John's mind they then became a particular group of men and he used the word *anér* (in one of its plural forms). The first occasion it was just "peoples" in his mind (as translated in NIV, NKJV, et al), so he used *anthrópos*.

When we look at the following two passages it will be further seen that the emphasis of *anér* on its own is "a particular man":

> Blessed is the man to whom the LORD shall not impute sin.
>
> *Romans 4:8*

> Blessed *is* the man who endures temptation . . .
>
> *James 1:12*

In both verses, the Greek word for "man" is *anér*. What is significant is that the Greek text in these does not contain the definite article "the" in front of *anér*. This is important as there is an appreciation of the fact that a particular person is understood, so that in English, the definite article needs to be added. This is a further indication to us, that by itself (without "the") *anér* has the emphasis of a particular person.

In 1 Corinthians 11:3, the word for "man" is *anér*, and it is found with the definite article "the" in front, which defines "the noun" as a distinct noun unlike "a noun" which could be any. Now, Greek does not have a separate word for the indefinite article "a, an", so it is added (at will) in translating when there is no definite article presented.

We are now ready to see what the following means in 1 Corinthians 11:3,

> . . . *kephalé-de gunaikos ho anér* . . .
>
> *1 Corinthians 11:3 Gk*

> . . . But head of a woman the [particular] man . . .
>
> *1 Corinthians 11:3 JM*

We know it is "of a woman" because the word *guné* is in its genitive form – the case of "belonging to/ offspring of". In English it is expressed by adding "of". Ephesians 5:23 is a good example showing *gunaikos* and *anér* with the same declensions as 1 Corinthians 11:3

> . . . hoti ho anér estin kephalé tés gunaikos, hós kai ho Christos kephalé tés ekklésias . . .
>
> *Ephesians 5:23Gk*

> . . . for the husband is head of the wife as also the Christ [is] head of the assembly . . .
>
> *Ephesians 5:23 JM*

So, I ask myself: Who is the particular man of a woman?

Answer: No one but her own husband.

And since *anér* is the Greek word from which to translate "husband", to avoid confusion 1 Corinthians 11:3 means:

> . . . and head of a woman the husband . . .
>
> *JM and The Amp.V, GNB1&2, RSV, LB*

This passage therefore does not mention a general headship of man over woman but only of a particular man over a woman: her husband.

It is of note that when Paul said "the head of every man is Christ" he does not continue with the head of every woman is the husband. Perhaps he was conscious that not every woman is married, but in his day was it not the norm for a woman to be married? Certainly, when he wrote to Timothy about widows he encouraged the younger to remarry thus pointing to such a norm (1 Timothy 5:14).

Numbers 30 gives us an indication that in Hebrew homes the head of the house was either the husband or the father of the unmarried woman. A good chapter too to give a pointer to man's unhelpful passivity in that if a woman makes a vow and the man says nothing, then her vow stands. In *Leadership is male?* I mention the two inherent weaknesses: one in man and one in woman before the first sin. Equally the widow and the divorced woman living on their own stood alone in what they vowed.

> But any vow of a widow or a divorced woman, by which she has bound herself, shall stand against her.
> *Numbers 30:9*

Just as these women alone stood before God and were responsible thus making the Lord their head, so today the unmarried woman stands with Christ as her head. 1 Corinthians 11:3 cannot be used therefore to understand a general headship of man over woman.

A comparison

Just as the Pharisees legalised and imposed a certain view and practise concerning the Sabbath which Jesus refuted by saying "The Sabbath was made for man, and not man for the Sabbath" (Mark 2:27), so also the creation order of woman being made after the man was done for the marriage's sake – as an example to the order of responsibility within it – and not for general functions between the genders. Which is why we also have the instruction "Wives submit to your own husbands" i.e. not someone else's husband (Ephesians 5:22, Colossians 3:18, 1 Peter 3:1).

The second passage to look in detail in regards to women in leadership now is 1 Timothy 2:12 (chapter 13).

> . . . and head of a woman the husband . . .
> *1 Corinthians 11:3 JM and The Amp.V,*
> *GNB1&2, RSV, LB*

ADDED WORDS AND
BAD CASE TRANSLATIONS

10

MARK 11:22

This bible text is the first I ever wrote about in relation to the way it is translated. I did this sometime in the early 90s and I originally entitled it *The interest of learning New Testament Greek* and submitted it as an article for inclusion in a church magazine. Later I re-produced the article as a web page and to help highlight the important truth the passage reveals that had been missing from the translation of the Greek, I re-named it *Have God's faith*.

Koïne Greek is the language of the New Testament. The word koïne means "common" and this was the common tongue – the lingua franca – of the region at the time. This is why the inscription upon the cross which Pilate had erected above Jesus was also written in Greek:

> And an inscription also was written over Him in letters of Greek, Latin, and Hebrew   *Luke 23:38*

Koïne Greek differs from English in many ways. One which stands out is the fact that the meaning of a sentence depends more on the relationship between words than their arrangement in the sentence.

I mentioned this in the previous chapter, but for all who have jumped to this chapter without reading the previous one I repeat: In English, the meaning will change with the order in which the words are placed: "An angel speaks to a man" has a different meaning to "A man speaks to an angel". The words are the same in both sentences, but their arrangement in the sentence is different. The meaning has changed by the different placement of the words. Syntax is about the arrangement of words and the study of it.

In Greek the placing of the words in a different order is not as important as the ending of the words. The word endings show the relationship of one word to another in the sentence. This is known as the inflection of a word. Morphology is the study of how the words appear.

An example of inflection which still exists in English is in the genitive case (the form of a word which shows a belonging to or offspring of – hence the English words genealogy and genus).

"The father's son" and "The girl's toy" show "'s" – an apostrophe plus an "s" – as the genitive ending in English of the words "father" and "girl" in these examples. This serves to show the relationship of "belonging to/offspring of" the son in regards to the father, and the toy in regards to the girl. This is an example of inflection of a word.

In Greek, the order of the words can change in a sentence without a change in the meaning.

For example "The son father's" or "The toy girl's" is a possible order (in Greek) because the ending of the words show the relationship between the words; not the order of the words in the sentence. They could equally be written, "The son of (the) father" and "The toy of (the) girl".

So, in John 1:36, in the New Testament Greek, we find John the Baptist exclaiming,

ho amnos tou theou – the Lamb of God *John 1:36*

Literally word for word this is "the lamb (of) the of God" i.e. The lamb (belonging to) The God.

The relationship between the words are shown by the endings "*-os*" and "*-ou*". *Theos* the word for God in the nominative case, when ending in "*ou*" in a sentence shows it is in the genitive case.

In English, "of" or " 's" has to be added to show that relationship – the genitive case. The ending of *amnos* (lamb), "*-os*" shows it is the subject in this clause – the nominative case. So that, if we were to find the following in the Greek:

ho theos tou amnou = The God of the lamb. This would mean "The lamb's God".

With all this in mind, when Jesus says to his disciples:

Echete pistin theou   *Mark 11:22*

Echete ["*ch*" in *echete* is pronounced "k" just like in "christ"]

Echete = You (2nd person plural) have – You grab hold of (You take for yourselves/you hold onto)

pistin = faith

theou = of God

Echete pistin theou = You have faith of God – Have God's faith.

Echete pistin theou – Remember, the "*-ou*" ending is the genitive case with the word "*theos*". This applies to 1st declension words like *amnos* and *theos*. This shows it is the faith of God – His type of faith – Jesus wants us to have. He is thus saying, Have God's kind of faith – The faith belonging to God – as shown also by the context, a faith that has no doubt in it. Not a quantity of faith, but a quality of faith Jesus is encouraging us to have. Let's set the scene.

> Now in the morning, as they passed by, they saw the fig tree dried up from the roots. And Peter, remembering, said to Him, "Rabbi, look! The fig tree which You cursed has withered away."
>
> So Jesus answered and said to them, "Have faith in God. For assuredly, I say to you, whoever says to this mountain, 'Be removed and be cast into the sea,' and does not doubt in his heart, but believes that those things he says will come to pass, he will have whatever he says. Therefore I say to you, whatever

things you ask when you pray, believe that you receive *them*, and you will have *them*.   Mark 11:20-24

The previous day as Jesus was making his way to the temple he had approached a fig tree to see if there was any fruit on it. There was not because it was not the season for fruit.

And seeing from afar a fig tree having leaves, He went to see if perhaps He would find something on it. And when He came to it, He found nothing but leaves, for it was not the season for figs. *Mark 11:13*

What Jesus did next is to curse the tree.

In response Jesus said to it, "Let no one eat fruit from you ever again."

And His disciples heard *it*.   Mark 11:14

So that the next day as they passed by again Peter mentioned that the tree Jesus had cursed was now already withering up. To which Jesus then exclaimed "Have God's faith" Have, for yourselves, God's kind of faith. For if you say to something to move and believe in your heart without doubt – just like God does – then it will be.

The word "in" as with, "have faith in God" in the NKJV does not exist in the Greek text, but this is the way the Greek has been translated in many

English versions. There is a Greek word for "in" it is *en* and this is not to be found in the Greek text for this verse. So here, we see a clear benefit of learning New Testament Greek. But, this is no excuse for seeing this mistranslated by those who claim to have learned the language (even to this basic amount).

The context of the passage itself gives us the encouragement to believe with this kind of faith.

> Therefore I say to you, whatever things you ask when you pray, believe that you receive *them*, and you will have *them*.
> *Mark 11:24*

Jesus here expands on his thinking about having quality of faith like God's faith.

So, brothers and sisters, let's *Echete pistin theou*

Yes, let's "Have God's faith"!

And let us see more answered prayers and more of God's work in our lives!

> And Jesus answering saith to them, 'Have faith of God'
> *Mark 11:22 Young*

> And Jesus answering them says, 'Have God's faith'
> *Mark 11:22 JM*

11

ROMANS 8:28

We saw in the earlier chapter about the "three measures of meal" parable the importance not to lose the meaning of a passage and that having done so because of the modernising of language a crucial word was not translated. This then rendered the parable impossible to be understood at all. Here I wish to explain how again the loss of meaning of a passage has occurred and instead of a word being left out one has been added which prevents the appreciation of the passage as originally meant. I hope to show that the added word forces a meaning foreign to the theme of the text.

> And we know that all things work together for good to those who love God, to those who are the called according to *His* purpose.   *Romans 8:28*

The added word in question "***His***" has been placed in italics by the default translation used in this book: The New King James Version. Thomas Nelson Inc the publishers are to be complimented for this ongoing practise of placing in italics words that are not in the original text. This is not a practise of all translators and without a note also to highlight that this is an addition nothing prevents the reader from believing this is how it should be. Here is the NASB (it's the same for the ASV):

> And we know that God causes all things to work together for good to those who love God, to those who are called according to His purpose.
>
> *Romans 8:28 NASB*

Here is the NIV:

> And we know that in all things God works for the good of those who love him, who have been called according to his purpose. *Romans 8:28 NIV*

Or among the declared paraphrases – Here the NLT:

> And we know that God causes everything to work together for the good of those who love God and are called according to his purpose for them.
>
> *Romans 8:28 NLT*

As expected here is the honest literal translation of Robert Young:

> And we have known that to those loving God all things do work together for good, to those who are called according to purpose *Romans 8:28 Young*

So what is so important about this added word? Why does it take away from the meaning of the passage?

To explain this let's look at the context. I will borrow from the following chapters: *Romans 8:28 In Context, The early Church Fathers and predestination* and *The Apostles Paul and Judas* of my book *So you think you're Chosen?* As well as from the script of my later YouTube video entitled *Paul's teaching of Conditional Predestination – Jacques More*.

In Romans 8:29-30 – the following verses – we read Paul mention predestination like this:

> . . . whom He foreknew, He also predestined . . . whom He predestined, these He also called; whom He called, these He also justified; and whom He justified, these He also glorified.   *Romans 8:29-30*

What is not seen when the context is excluded is how this is Paul's teaching of conditional predestination. What helps prevent seeing conditional predestination is the added word "*His*" in Romans 8:28. I will now explain step by step how the foreknowledge is gained within the lifetime of the person, but is a knowledge gained ahead of that person's own knowledge of what is needful: hence the word *fore*knowledge mentioned by Paul (my emphasis). I will explain what the knowledge is that is obtained by God – as explicit in the text – it is of the love of God seen in the heart, after God has searched the heart of the person: and that to all those seen loving God, all things are then worked into good as expanded upon in Romans 8:29-30.

In Romans 8:29-30 we read a list of verbs which are at the core of understanding Paul's thinking about predestination. Romans 8:29 God foreknows. Romans 8:29-30 God predestines. Romans 8:30 God calls, God Justifies and God Glorifies. Paul lists these verbs in a particular order: Romans 8:29 – Whom He foreknew, He also predestined. Romans 8:30 – Whom He predestined, these He also called: Whom He called, these He also justified: Whom He justified, these He also glorified.

We see then before God predestines, before God makes a decision involving a destiny, knowledge is involved. So this knowledge is first and never after a decision to destine the person.

But, this is a decision about what? And this knowledge what kind is it? It is knowledge of what?

We see "to justify" is included in this list of verbs. This indicates that the destiny is about salvation. Paul earlier in this same letter had already mentioned:

> . . . being justified freely by His grace through the redemption that is in Christ Jesus . . . *Romans 3:24*

To justify then is about salvation. So predestination here is a decision about the destiny of the person involving salvation. What about the knowledge?

What knowledge? It reads "**whom He foreknew**", so the person is foreknown. But, again what specific is known about the person?

For that answer we need to be attached and fully connected to the preceding verses. If we are to understand Paul here, we cannot if we are divorced from following his train of thought: A text out of context is a pretext. We find the previous mention of knowledge God has about the person in Verses 27 and 28. Verses 29-30 are fully connected by the fact this is knowledge of the person in view. Paul expands about what God does with that knowledge in Romans 8:29-30. But what the knowledge is needs to be learned by seeing what Paul is saying 1st. In Verse 27 we read about an action of God:

Now He who searches the hearts . . .   *Romans 8:27*

God searches men's hearts. But, what is God looking for in the heart? We find this in Romans 8:28,

. . . to those who love God . . .   *Romans 8:28*

Here we see loving God in the heart is what is in view. So the searching of the heart is to see if the person loves God. The knowledge involved about the person is the fact that they love God.

When was this knowledge gained? Answer: when God searched the heart. Can God search a heart before a person exists? No.

How do we know this? How do we know that God always searches the heart of people who are actually living and breathing? Because that is how He does it throughout the bible.

> And you shall remember that the LORD your God led you all the way these forty years in the wilderness, to humble you *and* test you, to know what *was* in your heart, whether you would keep His commandments or not. *Deuteronomy 8:2*

When was this testing to know what was in the heart of the people of Israel? Answer: During 40 years of being in the wilderness.

> However, *regarding* the ambassadors of the princes of Babylon, whom they sent to him to inquire about the wonder that was *done* in the land, God withdrew from him, in order to test him, that He might know all *that was* in his heart. *2 Chronicles 32:31*

When was this testing of King Hezekiah for God to know? Answer: During the visit of the ambassadors. When God says to Abraham:

> Now I know that you fear God, since you have not withheld your son, your only *son*, from Me.
> *Genesis 22:12*

When was this testing? Answer: When Abraham was seen to go through the sacrificing of Isaac his son, which God prevented at the point of seeing Abraham was going through with it. God testing the heart is important in the bible:

> I, the LORD, search the heart, *I test* the mind, even to give every man according to his ways, and according to the fruit of his doings . . .　　　*Jeremiah 17:10*

> For the righteous God tests the hearts and minds.
> 　　　　　　　　　　　　　　　　　*Psalm 7:9*

> . . . I am He who searches the minds and hearts. And I will give to each one of you according to your works.　　　　　　　　　*Revelation 2:23*

But when God searches the heart is in a person's lifetime. So when we read God *fore*knows (my emphasis): Why is that? If this knowledge of loving God is gained in the lifetime of the person, why is it called foreknowledge?

It is because – again in context: carefully following Paul's train of thought - We see that the person is seen *not* to know what to pray for.

> . . . For we do not know what we should pray for as we ought . . .　　　　　　　　　*Romans 8:26*

"**The saints**" (V. 27) – like the O.T. saints i.e. pre-Christian – do not know what to "**pray for**" (V.26) at this stage of Paul's description. Namely at

117

this point in time they do not know to pray, "**to be conformed to the image of His Son**" (V.29) that is, until they are "**justified**" (V.30) which happens by knowing that "**redemption that is in Christ Jesus**" (Romans 3:24) and which occurs after they are "**called**" (V.28 and 30).

So what do we read? We read that: God knows after searching the heart – in the person's lifetime – that the person loves God before the person themselves knows what to pray. So the text in sequence reveals foreknowledge is about God knowing ahead of the person themselves knowing.

This helps makes sense of Romans 8:28 – Here follows a Greek to English interlinear step by step rendition:

Oidamen-de hoti tois agapósin ton theon panta sunergei eis agathon tois kata prothesin klétois ousin.   *Romans 8:28 Gk.*

Oidamen de – but we know
Hoti – that/because/since
Tois - to/for the ones
Agapósin – they are loving/they love
Ton theon – (the) God
Panta – all (things)
Sunergei – he/she/it works
Eis agathon – into good
Tois – to/for the ones
Kata (+ Accusative) – according to

Prothesin – (a) purpose (in the Accusative)/display of intent
Klétois – (to/for the ones) called
Ousin – they are

> But we know that He works all things into good for the ones loving God for they are the ones called according to a purpose.　　　*Romans 8:28 JM*

The purpose then is the loving of God seen in the heart.

Now *prothesis* = purpose – is the word used in Hebrews 9:2

Interlinear – *kai hé prothesis tón artón* – And the presentation of the loaves

> For a tabernacle was prepared: the first *part*, in which *was* the lampstand, the table, and the showbread, which is called the sanctuary . . .　　　*Hebrews 9:2*

This "presentation of the loaves" is often shortened to "*show*bread" (my emphasis). So *prothesis* is about the "showing", the "presentation". Robert Young's concordance defines *prothesis* as "A setting before, purpose". See also appendix 6 which outlines all the places where *prothesis* is found in the LXX.

And what was being displayed after God had searched the heart?

Answer: The loving of God.

This is the purpose in view – the display of intent – and according to that Paul says God then works all things into good. This is what is then expanded upon by Paul in Romans 8:29-30

Paul wrote: Whom God foreknew, He also predestined. Whom He predestined, these He also called. Whom He called, these He also justified. Whom He justified, these He also glorified (Romans 8:29-30).

Do you really believe Paul is speaking of something divorced from the preceding verses?

The introduction of "His" in Romans 8:28 removes the purpose in view: the loving of God in the heart of the saint. Adding "His" alludes to a purpose of God: one other than seen in the flow of the text. Incidentally Paul here calls anyone a saint as someone seen loving God in the heart before they know how to pray or to become a Christian – knowing how to pray: the specifics of what to pray for – to be conformed to the image of His Son (Romans 8:29) involves becoming a Christian. This is where the calling comes in: one is set up – predestined – to a calling to believe and know Jesus as your saviour and Lord.

Paul's conversion
A good example of this is how Paul came to be a Christian.

Paul mentions in the book of Romans that he had not known sin except for the law.

> . . . I would not have known sin except through the law. *Romans 7:7*

> . . . by the law *is* the knowledge of sin. *Romans 3:20*

If it was not for the law he would be ignorant of sin. He also mentions that there is "law" which is written in the heart.

> . . . when Gentiles, who do not have the law, by nature do the things *contained* in the law, these, although not having the law, are a law to themselves, who show the work of the law written in their hearts . . . *Romans 2:14-15*

This internal law, when violated, results in conscience accusing the offender.

> . . . their conscience also bearing witness, and between themselves *their* thoughts accusing or else excusing *them* . . . *Romans 2:15*

Thus Paul advocates for doing what you know to be right. He is also aware that you can do wrong without knowing that what you are doing is wrong.

> . . . I did *it* ignorantly in unbelief. *1 Timothy 1:13*

You can do wrong in the belief that it is not: by doing an act in ignorance that it is in itself not right. Paul's own persecution of the first Christians is a clear case in point. Paul did this in a time of ignorance: without knowledge that this was wrong. To him, at that point in time, not to persecute the Christians was to allow the name of his God and his religion to be defiled. His conscience as it was at that point would not be clear if he did not persecute Christians. The "law" and thus the knowledge of wrongdoing in this activity was not present in his heart and mind: Which is why he can tell us after having become a Christian and an apostle of Christ that his conscience had been clear before God and man (up) to that day.

> . . . I have lived in all good conscience before God
> until this day.   *Acts 23:1*

There was no envy in his heart out of which he persecuted Christ, unlike the way the Pharisees and other religious leaders had done. As Pilate declared when the religious leaders were accusing Jesus:

> For he knew that because of envy they had delivered
> Him.   *Matthew 27:18*

Which is why Jesus said to Paul:

> . . . *it is* hard for you . . .   *Acts 9:5*

Paul was already God's man for this was his honest purpose "before God". He had not violated any law that he knew of concerning what was wrong. The moment that he learned and was no longer ignorant concerning the fact that persecuting Christians was in fact attacking the very Lord he was trying to serve, he was no longer free by conscience to do this act against the law (in his heart): The law he had now learned. Of course by using the word "law" I use the same expression that Paul uses, but in modern day thinking the word "truth" may be more appropriate. The moment Paul had gained the truth that acts against Christians were acts against God, his conscience would no longer be clear were he to go on fighting them. However until that truth was real to him, his belief was that not to persecute Christians was to allow tainting of the religion of his fathers. He believed the God of the Torah was blasphemed by the followers of "the way". So his heart which was zealous for God would not permit him to rest whilst this "heresy" was propagated. Paul said that,

> . . . where there is no law *there is* no transgression.
> *Romans 4:15*

And that,

> . . . sin is not imputed [taken account of] when there
> is no law.   *Romans 5:13*

So it can be seen that until Paul learned the truth that his persecuting acts were wrong, until he understood transgression was involved, though he was committing sin, God who knew his heart motive was not holding it against him. That sin was not taken account of until there was knowledge of the truth that it was wrong. Paul's heart was so much for his God that his heart's prayer was to be able to follow God. God saw this and he thereby arranged:

1. Paul to go away from Jerusalem by his trip to Damascus and thus away from those persecuting Christ with the wrong motives.
2. Paul to be challenged on the road to Damascus and thus,
3. Paul to be set free and healed to follow God more fully just as his heart desired.

> For whoever has, to him more will be given, and he will have abundance; but whoever does not have, even what he has will be taken away from him.
>
> *Matthew 13:12*

So God having tested Paul's heart (R8:27) knew that Paul loved Him. But that Paul did not know what to pray (R8:26). So with this foreknowledge – ahead of Paul – God worked all things into good (R8:28) in order to conform Paul to the image of His Son (R8:29). Namely, he set Paul up – He predestined him (R8:29) – to a call on the road to Damascus following which his repentance on learning he was doing wrong and acceptance of Jesus as his Lord, he was then justified (R8:30). And in his ongoing persecution as a follower of Christ as we who suffer with Him will – we are promised to share in his reign and glory (R8:17; 2 Timothy 2:12; R8:30).

The added word

The word "His" added in front of "purpose" in Romans 8:28 takes the reader away from seeing the purpose in the heart of the individual. This is against the flow of the developing text of Paul and superimposes the thinking that God's purpose is in view. The earliest example of this inclusion is in the Latin Vulgate which Jerome began to compile. Jerome corresponded for 25 years with Augustine of Hippo and this translation from the Greek into Latin became the main bible in the Western Roman Empire and for all Latin speakers. So that at the time of the Reformation and move away from the Western Church which mainly comprised of the Roman Catholic church, the new translations of the bible as used in the new denominations followed this earlier translation in continuing to add "His" in the text. Augustine is the originator of the belief system that "free will is not" when up to the time of his writings the universal doctrine was that of synergism – God and man co-operate. Synergism is seen in the above explanation of Romans 8:28 as seen in context and history shows this was the universal orthodoxy in the Church prior to Augustine.

> In harmony with the foregoing views as to human freedom and responsibility, *conditional predestination is the doctrine inculcated by the Greek Fathers.*
>
> *History of Christian Doctrine* p.165 George Park Fisher DD LLD - T&T Clark *(Italics mine)*

Inculcated means it was the teaching urged or impressed persistently by the early Church Fathers. Conditional means in God's desire for you, if you work with Him it will happen; if you don't want Him, it cannot happen. Which, of course, is true due to His Self control (Galatians 5:23). Immediately preceding this statement, but after his various quotes from the Early Church Fathers, Prof. Fisher states:

> . . . the renewal of the soul is made to be the result of the factors, divine grace and the exertion of man's free-will. As a rule, the exertion of free-will, human efforts in a right direction, precede the divine aid, and render men worthy of it. It is a doctrine of synergism. God and man cooperate. *ibid.* p.165

> But we know that He works all things into good for the ones loving God for they are the ones called according to a purpose. *Romans 8:28 JM*

Due to the history – the long use of the added word – a note added to this verse would be a reasonable practise to expect from translators alongside the removal of "His": N.B. The purpose in view is the loving of

126

God in the heart of the individual following God's searching as per verse 27. Alternatively, bearing in mind the root meaning of *prothesis* involves "a showing" (see Appendix 6) a fuller translation of *prothesis* is appropriate:

> But we know that He works all things into good for the ones loving God for they are the ones called according to a displayed intent. *Romans 8:28 JM*

12

EPHESIANS 2:1

In this chapter in the added word and bad case translation category we find that the word "in" is not translated from the very Greek equivalent *en* but is there as a result of the grammatical case of the words in the passage. This is not a problem except that the word "in" is insufficient alone in fully translating what is meant by its addition. This incomplete transmission would not be so important were it not for this verse being regularly used as a proof text to advocate an alleged truth which appears to be so by the misuse of the word "in". The dogma advocated by this proof text is in fact contradicted by the very passage when understood how "in" is applicable within the translation.

> And you *He made alive*, who were dead in trespasses
> and sins,   *Ephesians 2:1*

This passage is read and used as a proof text to mean that before becoming Christians all are dead spiritually and thus unable to turn to God without His bringing spiritual life to them. Note how the NKJV has placed "***He made alive***" in italics to show that these words are not in the Greek and indeed is not part of the flow of the text. To quickly illustrate here is Young's literal version:

> Also you – being dead in the trespasses and the
> sins, *Ephesians 2:1 Young*

These added words are no help as by them the emphasis is taken away from the act of sinning which as per the ongoing context can be seen as what Paul was emphasizing. Instead the emphasis is placed on the death itself since mentioning life from God highlights its opposite: death. Paul goes on about the sin not the death.

> [sin] in which you once walked according to the
> course of this world . . . *Ephesians 2:2*

Now, what is also useful in Young is his translating of the definite article "**the**" in front of "**trespasses**" and in front of "**sins**". This helps make a closer appreciation of the reason "**in**" is there. It is WHILST IN the trespasses and the sins that the death mentioned is applicable (my emphasis). The reason for this emphasis is that the Greek for *en* which is the equivalent for the English "in" is not in the Greek in this verse. Instead we find the words "**the trespasses and the sins**" are found in the Dative case.

> Kai humas ontas nekrous tois paraptómasin kai tais
> hamartiais,   *Ephesians 2:1*

Here we see "**Kai humas**" And you, "**ontas nekrous**"
being dead, "**tois paraptómasin kai tais hamartiais**"
– then word for word – the trespasses and the sins.
These last words are in the Dative (with the exception
of the conjunction "**kai**" and, of course.

We can see "in" from *en* in the next Verse.

> En hais pote periepatésate – in which once ye did
> walk   *Ephesians 2:2 Greek - Young*

Here we have "**En hais pote**" in which once,
"**periepatésate**" you walked. So why, you may ask is
"in" found in translations of Ephesians 2:1?

It is because the death mentioned – the separation
from the life of God – occurs whilst in the practise
of the sins and the trespasses. The use of the Dative
here is known as the instrumental use of the Dative.
It is the means by which something occurs or comes
about. So that it is only whilst in trespasses and sins
that death applies. Death as separation from God is
due to the practise of sin. Like a cloud that separates
us from the sun, sin separates us from God. A good
mention of this reality is in Isaiah:

> I have blotted out, like a thick cloud, your trans-
> gressions, and like a cloud, your sins. Return to Me,
> for I have redeemed you.   *Isaiah 44:22*

And, just as the sin is what separates, the ceasing from sin enables renewed relationship with God. In Ephesians 2:1 the fact that the death is only there by the means of the practise of sins and trespasses indicates that the ceasing from sin is what permits life – a lack of separation. In the Greek reading Ephesians 2:1 indicates the existence of an inherent ability to either cease or to remain in the practise of sin. Death is as a result of something is explicit. Death is not there through another's sin but one's own active sin and if persisted. It is needful therefore to consider ways to translate or add a note so that such unfit proof text practise can be limited. This is why Young's use of the definite article is helpful.

> . . . being dead in the trespasses and the sins
> *Ephesians 2:1 Young*

It is whilst in "the" trespasses and "the" sins that the death occurs. So if the definite article is not translated then adding "whilst" is another way to show this. It needs not to be put in italics as it is a fuller translation of an existing meaning of the instrumental use of the Dative.

> And you – being dead whilst in trespasses and sins,
> *Ephesians 2:1 JM*

Now, there are other uses of the Dative that could be argued as relevant here. A Locative use which would make no difference as it would still mean that it is whilst located in the middle of sin and trespasses that death was existing. Even if a causal (or Motive) use could be seen, this in effect is the same as instrumental here as the reason for death is the practise of sinning and trespassing.

Examples of the instrumental use of the Dative are plentiful – here are two passages:

> ékraxen phoné melagé – he cried with a loud voice
> *Acts 7:60 Greek - Young*

Here we have "**ékraxen**" he cried, followed by "**phoné**" voice, and "**melagé**" loud, both "voice" and "loud" are in the Dative, the instrumental use is recognised and applied by adding "**with**" in the translation. Equally if the word "in" was used as opposed to "with" within the phrase "in a loud voice", it would mean the same (See also Acts 7:57a).

Note: The Dative here is not shown by the ending of the words, but by the accent below the last letter of these and this is not shown in the English representation of the Greek letters as that is not included in this book's system of Greek letter representation.

> Maria hé aleipsasa ton kurion muró - Mary who did anoint the Lord with ointment
> *John 11:2a Greek - Young*

Here we have "**Maria hé aleipsasa ton kurion**" Mary who anointed the Lord, followed by "**muró**" fragrant oil or ointment, in the Dative, the instrumental use is recognised and applied by adding "**with**" in the translation. The previous paragraph's note about the Dative recognised by the accent also applies.

> Kai ekmaxasa tous podas autou tais thrixin autés
> - and did wipe his feet with her hair
>
> *John 11:2b Greek - Young*

Here the passage continues with "**Kai ekmaxasa tous podas autou**" word for word "and wiped the feet of his", followed by "**tais thrixin autés**" the hair of her. This is with "the hair" in the Dative, the instrumental use is recognised and applied also by adding "**with**" in the translation. These examples are recognised and known as examples of the instrumental use of the Dative.

Now, the Dative is used most commonly to denote the indirect object of a verb – the object or person "to" or "for" something is done, just as the Accusative most commonly denotes the direct object of a verb – the object or person involved in the action. But, except for particular prepositions like "in" translated from the Greek word *en* or a few verbs like "I believe" *pisteuó* that take the Dative, and similarly minor examples, then as exampled, the Dative reflects a relationship between words or clauses.

Here follows 3 English translations and 1 French one that express well the means by which they were dead:

And you did he make alive, when ye were dead
through your trespasses and sins,
American Standard Version

Once you were dead because of your disobedience
and your many sins.   *New Living Translation*

Vous étiez morts par vos offenses et par vos péchés,
Louis Segond (1910)

Lit. You were dead by your offences and by your sins.

And you – being dead whilst in trespasses and sins,
Ephesians 2:1 JM

13

1 TIMOTHY 2:12

As per the intro to the chapter on 1 Corinthians 11:3 I have adapted this chapter from the one of the same name in the book *Leadership is male?*

In the 1 Corinthians 11:3 Chapter I mentioned three passages of the New Testament as being the likely candidates for the reasoning of the late John Wimber of Vineyard Christian Fellowships for not having women involved in the top government of the church. I mentioned this was likely to consist of passages within 1 Corinthians 11, 1 Corinthians 14 and 1 Timothy 2. I dealt with 1 Corinthians 11 as encapsulated by verse 3 and the reasons were given to show that this was best translated as follows:

> . . . and head of a woman the husband . . .
>
> *1 Corinthians 11:3 JM*
> *As also translated this way by the Amp.V,*
> *GNB1&2, RSV, LB*

This accurate rendering as outlined in the chapter removes the passage from use as an indication that there is a general male headship over woman. We are now left with 1 Corinthians 14 and 1 Timothy 2. The verses in detail are 1 Corinthians 14:34 and 1 Timothy

2:12. What are we to make of these passages? Timothy is probably the most used and seemingly clear-cut text to forbid women involvement in church leadership or teaching:

> And I do not permit a woman to teach or to have authority over a man, but to be in silence.
>
> *1 Timothy 2:12*

On its own this passage seems quite sufficient to advocate male leadership. Paul does not permit women to teach and further, any exercise of authority over a man is forbidden. Certainly this is what is written in this "sound byte" of many translations.

Now, a reading of the immediate context and, particularly when this is done directly from the Greek, a limitation shows up as divergent with this thinking. This would contradict the immediate appearance mentioned. In the Greek text, verse 11 is not separate from verse 12 but sets the scene for it. Verse 12 is an extension, not a separate command. Verse 11 states:

> Let a woman learn in silence with all submission.
>
> *1 Timothy 2:11*

So what we have is an exhortation not to allow – by Paul's own example "I do not permit" – women to teach or bear authority, but only when in a learning situation. This is re-emphasised by Paul then mentioning afresh the attitude "to be in silence": in other words the first words of the sentence (in V.11 in the Greek), "a woman in quietness" and the last words of the same sentence (in V.12) are "in quietness." Paul is using the same phrase at the beginning and at the end: *en hésuchia* – in quietness.

The immediate setting therefore encapsulated at front and end by this phrase "in quietness" shows this is dealing with a public learning situation. And to show these sentences are together both the learning context and the injunction are sandwiched by the same phrase: Clearly confirming the immediate setting:

> A woman in quietness/silence . . . but to be in quietness/silence.   *1 Timothy 2:11-12 JM*

Here are verses 11-12 in the Greek:

> *Guné - en - hésuchia - manthanetó – en – pasé –*
> *hupotagé.* * *gunaiki – de – didaskein – ouk –*
> *epitrepó,* * *oude – authentein – andros,* – all' –
> *einai – en – hésuchia.*   *1 Timothy 2:11-12 Greek*

To help show how this literally translates here follows the two verses in full and please note that dashes are to help follow the direct translation as are the asterisks * (used here at the so-called "punctuation" breaks of the Greek Text – N.B. very early extant manuscripts have no space in between words nor punctuations):

(a) woman/wife - in - quietness/silence - learn let
(her) - in - all - submissiveness/subjection; * to/for
(a) woman/wife - but/and – to teach/instruct -
not - I allow/permit, * nor – to have/exercise
authority – of (a) man/husband, - but – to be - in -
quietness/silence.

In quietness let a woman learn in all submissive-
ness; and I do not allow for a woman to teach, nor
to exercise authority of a husband, but to be in
quietness.   *1 Timothy 2:11-12 JM*

Let a woman learn in silence with all submission.
And I do not permit a woman to teach or to have
authority over a man, but to be in silence.
                            1 Timothy 2:11-12 NKJV

As can be seen there are a few differences between
my direct translation and that of the NKJV. Some of
the translation done on 1 Timothy 2:12 has been
overlooked or, left undone by the majority of Bible
translations (I have looked at 27 to date), there is
therefore the need to demonstrate the authenticity of
my rendering:

1. Of the versions I have observed only 4 translate
   the word "woman/wife" in its second mention
   in the passage with its dative (the grammatical
   form of the word showing impersonal/third party
   interest) [2 French versions, 1 interlinear and

The Jerusalem Bible]: In English this is done by adding "to" or "for". guné is the word as the subject of a verb – the nominative case, in the text it is gunaiki the Dative case. An example of what I mean is Matthew 19:5.

Kataleipsei - anthrópos – ton – patera – kai – tén - métera, * kai – proskolléthésetai – té – **gunaiki** - autou,   *Matthew 19:5*

(he) shall leave – (a) man – the – father – and – the – mother, * and – (he) shall be joined – the – **to/for (a) wife/woman** – of his,

. . . a man shall leave his father and mother and be joined **to** his **wife** . . .   *Matthew 19:5 NKJV*

All I want to show here is that *gunaiki* means "to a wife/woman" or, "for a wife/woman".

2. Only 3 versions translate the word *anér* "man/ husband" in its genitive case (the grammatical form showing "genus") and they are all interlinear translations. In English this is done by adding "of" or "'s" to the noun in question. *Andra* is the form of the word as a direct recipient or object of the verb – accusative case, in the text is *andros* the genitive case. On this part of the translation I wish to spend some time due to the importance to the whole meaning. Here follows

141

the examples of the genitive simple use of *anér* in the New Testament. There are other uses of the genitive, I cover there in appendix 4.

Andros
All emphasis added is mine (so the reader can see what he is looking at)

1. . . . who were born, not of blood, nor of the will of the flesh, nor of the will **of man**, but of God.
   John 1:13

   . . . *hoi – ouk – ex – haimatón - oude - ek – thelématos - sarkos - oude - ek - thelématos - **andros** - all' – ek - THeou – egennéthésan.*

   . . . the - not - out of/from - bloods - nor - out of/from - will - of flesh - nor - out of/from - will - **of (a) man -** but - out of/from - God - (they) were born.

2. For the woman who has a husband is bound by the law to *her* husband as long as he lives. But if the husband dies, she is released from the law **of** *her* **husband**.
   Romans 7:2

   hé – gar – hupandros – guné – tó – zónti – andri – dedetai – nomó. * ean – de – apothané – ho – anér – katérgétai – apo – tou – nomou – tou – **andros**.

   the – for – married [by a husband] – (a) woman – to the – living – husband – is bound

142

by – law; * if – but – should die – the – husband
– she is cleared – from – the – law – of the –
(of a) husband.

3. But I want you to know that the head **of** every
man is Christ, the head of woman *is* man, and
the head of Christ is God.   *1 Corinthians 11:3*
*(See the separate chapter for a more
accurate rendering)*

*THeló –de – humas – eidenai, * hoti – pantos
– **andros** – hé – kephalé – ho – CHristos –
estin. * kephalé – de – gunaikos – ho – anér.
* kephalé –de – CHristou, * ho – THeos.*

I wish – but – you – to know, * that – of every –
(of a) man – the – head – the – Christ – he is;
* head – but – of a woman – the – husband; *
head – but – of Christ, * [the] – God.

4. For a man indeed ought not to cover *his* head,
since he is the image and glory of God; but
woman is the glory **of man**. *1 Corinthians 11:7*

*Anér – men – gar – ouk – opheilei –
katakaluptesthai – tén – kephalén, * eikón –
kai – doxa – THeou – huparchón. * Guné –
de – doxa – **andros** – estin.*

Man – indeed – for – not – he ought – to have
covered – the – head, * image – and – glory – of
God – being; * woman – but – glory – **of a
husband** – she is;

5. Do not let a widow under sixty years old be taken into the number, *and not unless* she has been the wife **of** one **man** . . .   *1 Timothy 5:9*

*CHéra – katalegesthó – mé – elatton – etón – exékonta – gegonuia, * enos – **andros** – guné,*

A widow – let be put in the list – not – less – years – sixty – being * of one – **(of a) husband** – (a) wife,

6 . . . for the wrath **of man** does not produce the righteousness of God.   *James 1:20*

*. . . orgé – gar – **andros** – dikaiosunén – THeou – ou – katergazetai.*

. . . wrath – for – **of a man** – righteousness – of God – not – works out.

The purpose of my display of these is to plainly show that the normal and basic use of *andros* is to say "of a man/a man's" or, "of a husband/a husband's".

These are the instances in the New Testament that *andros* is found. This is just the word *anér* "a [particular] man" or, "a husband" in the genitive. These examples refer to the genitive use in the singular. The plural form is *andrón*. The instances given are the simple use of the genitive which involves the case of belonging to or being the offspring of. In English this is done by adding the apostrophe: e.g. a man's wife or, by adding "of": e.g. of the husband. All other instances of *andros* and their uses as well as all the instances in plural are given at the end of the 4th Appendix – *Anér*.

As mentioned my purpose in displaying these examples is to show the reader the normal use of the genitive of *anér*. *Andros* is correctly translated "of a man", "of a husband" or, "a man's", "a husband's". In Greek there is no separate word for the indefinite article "a" or "an" so this is added or omitted purely by inclination. Just as with *guné* the word for "a wife" or "a woman" is like the French "femme" and can mean either "wife" or "woman" dependent on context. As we also saw in the 1 Corinthians 11:3 chapter, when it is meant for "a man" the common use-age reveals it is meant of "a particular man" because *anér* is being used and not *anthròpos*. So that you can now see that my translation of 1 Timothy 2:12 is perfectly reasonable as follows:

> And I do not allow for a woman to teach, nor to exercise authority of a husband, but to be in quietness.   *1 Timothy 2:12 JM*

It is of course important to note also that if I wanted to say "of a husband", there is no other way for me to do so than by just *andros* in the Greek.

Now, in view of the preceding chapters within the book *Leadership is male?* explaining God's instruction to Eve to submit her desire to her husband to decide about – for her safety from deception – then it makes full sense to translate as "To exercise authority of a husband" from *authentein andros*. Why? Because that is the authority given to the husband in the one flesh relationship and in a learning setting a woman should not exercise that "teaching" or "authority" due to the deception factor. I could translate this as "to exercise authority of a man", but since *anér* means "a particular man" if "husband" is in doubt, and since the authority alluded to, I explain as referring to the marriage – the one flesh partnership – then, I think it good and accurate to use the word "husband". Also I have highlighted the authority of a husband from God's words in Genesis 3:16 and why this was so, earlier on in that book, it makes no sense thereby to translate other than "husband".

My reasoning for translating *guné* above as "woman" is confined to the fact that *guné* – in the dative case here: *gunaiki* – is the Greek word from which to translate "wife" and "woman" and the understanding is that it is the gender as a whole and not individual wives who are susceptible with that kind of deception, as Eve was. Paul speaks of what he allows for the gender. It is not about wives, but all women in the assembly during this learning time only. This is not a time Paul allows for women to interact or teach from the floor, but to be in quietness.

For the understanding of *authentein* being understood as "to exercise authority" I refer the reader to Appendix 7 – *AUTHENTEÓ*

Recap

My reasoning for translating "husband" is confined to the fact that *anér* – in the genitive case here: *andros* – is the only Greek word from which to translate "husband". It is also due to Paul's ensuing reasoning for the statement he has just made. In verses 13-14 Paul lays his reason upon the creation order and the authority of responsibility a husband has been given to him. This authority to rule over (in a certain context) was as a result of the fall initiated by the deception Eve played a part in (Genesis 3:16b) as I explain in the earlier chapters of *Leadership is male?* This is not a general authority to all men over all women, but to a particular man over his wife in the Lord: Which is why Paul also states elsewhere "wives submit to your own husbands, as to the Lord." (Ephesians 5:22): i.e. not somebody else's husband. The authority is the husband's not any other man's. Of course with this translation now in hand it is important to appreciate why Paul said all this and it is safer to repeat that I believe any book on that topic which does not explain the deception difference between men and women does not actually address what Paul was talking about.

> And I do not allow for a woman to teach, nor to exercise authority of a husband, but to be in quietness. *1 Timothy 2:12 JM*

DOCTRINAL BIAS
IN TRANSLATIONS

14

SUCH AS SHOULD BE SAVED

An example of theological bias in translation

In this chapter I will give an example of theological bias in translation. The KJV is highly regarded through much of its history. What is not so well known is the divergence from the Greek in the translation to give a deliberate interpretation that forces Calvinist dogma into the reading. Calvinism is the common name for reformed doctrine or unconditional predestination teaching that was re-asserted in the Reformation period of the 16th century not least by John Calvin, hence the name Calvinism. I say re-asserted as it was introduced in the church by Augustine in the 5th century and unknown before that. The doctrinal bias in the translation was carried out through the use of Theodore Beza's version of the Greek Text and his many translation notes. Beza was Calvin's successor in Geneva where Calvin resided and ruled and he was an ardent promoter of that theology. This dogma thoroughly flavoured all his writings and it is his influence upon the translation of the Greek text that has come into the KJV.

For the unfamiliar reader Calvinism is the theology that God alone is the initiator and means by which anyone goes on to obtain and then retain their faith against the persistent teaching prior to Augustine of synergism where God and man co-operate. "Free-will is not" began with Augustine. This theology is better known in terms of the idea that God has chosen all He wants saved and all He wants lost from the foundation of the world: that all are predestined to the eternal fate God chose for them. This is Calvinism in its simplest form and fully attested by Calvin's principal work *Institutes of the Christian Religion*. And it is this idea that is explicit in the translation of the Greek in the KJV. This is well seen in Acts 2:47 even though, as you shall see, the very same Greek grammar is translated correctly elsewhere in the KJV in a place where the doctrine mentioned is not in view.

> . . . the Lord added to the church daily such as *should be saved*.
>
> *Acts 2:47 KJV Italics and extra emphasis mine*

As mentioned italics are mine and indeed throughout I have put in bold and enlarged what is needful.

This "***should be saved***" gives a clear implication that there are some who "should not be saved" and that it was only those thus designated that the Lord added to the church.

Is this a correct translation of the Greek text?

Do other versions translate this portion of Scripture this way?

The Greek is as follows:

Ho – de - Kurios – prosetithei - tous - sózomenous - kath hémeran – té - ekklésia

The – but - Lord – (he) added - the (ones) – [who] were being saved - daily - to the - church

As can be seen the portion at issue is *sózomenous* a form of the verb *sózó*, "I save". Let us look at a range of other versions and see how they compare:

. . . the Lord added to the church daily those who were being saved.   *NKJV*

. . . the Lord added to their number daily those who were being saved.   *NIV*

. . . added to them day by day those that were being saved.   *RV*

. . . added to their number day by day those who were being saved.   *RSV*

. . . added to their group those who were being saved.   *GNB*

. . . added to their number those who were finding salvation.   *J.B. Phillips*

. . . and the Lord was adding those being saved every day to the assembly.   *Young*

153

I have just quoted from at least 7 English versions of the Bible and I have more which say the same including 4 different Greek-English Interlinear versions.

There are other places where the verb "to save" is found *in the same tense* and it is significant that here the KJV does not translate it "should" along with its implication.

1 Corinthians 1:18

> *tois de sózomenois hémin dunamis theou estin*
> *1 Corinthians 1:18*

Because the "tense" is a Participle – a verbal adjective qualifying a noun but keeping some properties of a verb – it is visible that the ending is different fractionally from *sózomenous* as in Acts 2:47. There the *-ous* agrees with *tous* = "the (ones)", but in the Corinthians passage *-ois* agrees with *tois* = "to/for the (ones)". Please notice how in no way this affects the translation of the sense of action – the tense – of the verbal part but only as to which noun it relates to: it is the adjective section of the participle which has changed. The tense is the same as in Acts 2:47 but here it is seen translated:

> . . . unto us which are saved it is the power of God.
> *KJV*

... to us who are being saved it is the power of God.

NKJV

... to us who are being saved it is the power of God.

NIV

No bias here in the same version that placed it in Acts 2:47.

2 Corinthians 2.15

> *hoti christou euódia esmen tó theó en tois sózomenois*　　　*2 Corinthians 2:15*

For we are unto God a sweet savour of Christ, in them that are saved ...　　　*KJV*

For we are to God the fragrance of Christ among those who are being saved ...　　　*NKJV*

For we are to God the aroma of Christ among those who are being saved ...　　　*NIV*

The word "should" is not a part of *sózó* and cannot be translated by it.

For the sentence to include this emphasis another verb *dei* would need to be added. Now that has the meaning of "ought", "it is necessary", "should", etc. But, as you can see it does not exist in the Greek text quoted above for Acts 2:47.

I have employed throughout the same Greek text – the Received Text - as employed by the translators of the KJV and this is a clear example of imposing a theological idea into the bible reading without warrant from the Greek grammar.

> The Lord added to the church daily those who were being saved. *Acts 2:47*

15

ACTS 18:27

In the preceding chapter I explain the doctrinal bias in the KJV in Acts 2:47 and demonstrate how a more accurate translation of the Greek in more modern versions have removed that bias. However the bias towards Calvinism continues in other passages in some modern versions. Acts 18:27 is one such example.

> And when he desired to cross to Achaia, the brethren wrote, exhorting the disciples to receive him; and when he arrived, he greatly helped those who had believed through grace; for he vigorously refuted the Jews publicly, showing from the Scriptures that Jesus is the Christ. *Acts 18:27-28*

This passage describes the gifted bible teacher Apollos helping through that ability the believers of the region. We can see this in the NKJV just quoted as the "grace" – the bible teaching ability mentioned in Verse 27 is then explained further in saying how Apollos helped:

> . . . for he vigorously refuted the Jews publicly, showing from the Scriptures that Jesus is the Christ. *Acts 18:28*

The Greek of Luke – the writer of the book of Acts – mentions "the grace" just as Paul also uses the term to mention gifts God gives to help the church in his letter to the Romans.

> For I say, through the grace given to me, to everyone who is among you . . .   *Romans 12:3*

In the same passage Paul goes on to mention further:

> Having then gifts differing according to the grace that is given to us, *let us use them* . . . *Romans 12:6*

So where is this bias in the translation of Acts 18:27? It is in versions like the NIV, the NLT and *The Message*.

> When Apollos wanted to go to Achaia, the brothers encouraged him and wrote to the disciples there to welcome him. On arriving, he was a great help to those who by grace had believed.   *Acts 18:27 NIV*

The sight of Apollos' teaching gift is not in view as "the grace" but instead the assertion is made that the belief of the disciples was a gift of God. "Grace" is a common name used in Reformed or Calvinist circles to describe that theology. Here in the NIV the word is not used as a mention of the gift Apollos had of teaching. The NIV emphasis is that it is the faith of the believers that was a gift. *The Message* calls this grace "God's immense generosity" but there too it is the fact that they had become believers in view and Apollos' gift of teaching is not seen.

> When Apollos decided to go on to Achaia province, his Ephesian friends gave their blessing and wrote a letter of recommendation for him, urging the disciples there to welcome him with open arms. The welcome paid off: Apollos turned out to be a great help to those who had become believers through God's immense generosity. He was particularly effective in public debate with the Jews as he brought out proof after convincing proof from the Scriptures that Jesus was in fact God's Messiah.
>
> *Acts 18:27-28 The Message*

The NLT is no better.

> Apollos had been thinking about going to Achaia, and the brothers and sisters in Ephesus encouraged him to go. They wrote to the believers in Achaia, asking them to welcome him. When he arrived there, he proved to be of great benefit to those who, by God's grace, had believed.   *Acts 18:27 NLT*

It may be that the very placing of the separation between verses 27 and 28 tends to stop the flow of words going on to explain what the grace in view was about: the gift of teaching which Apollos possessed.

Quoting the two verses together from Young it is easier to view the "for" following the "grace" as it expands on the theme being conveyed.

> and he being minded to go through into Achaia, the brethren wrote to the disciples, having exhorted them to receive him, who having come, did help them much who have believed through the grace, for powerfully the Jews he was refuting publicly, shewing through the Writings Jesus to be the Christ.
>
> *Acts 18:27-28 Young*

USE OF NOTES
IN TRANSLATIONS

16

USE OF NOTES IN TRANSLATIONS

The NKJV makes use of italics in two main ways in the formatting of characters of words in a text of the bible. Throughout the Old and New Testament words not found in the original but added by the translator have been placed in italics. The addition is to better help the flow and often the meaning is also helped by this addition. The other main way italics are used is to show that the words are part of a quote of the Old Testament made in the New Testament. So that in effect the translator by the use of a different font character has added to the translation a kind of note to the text to assist the reader in his appreciation of the text.

Optional
A useful bible study aid in adding notes are references to other bible passages that are about the same topic. This is an optional aid, but a very useful one. Historical anecdotes or explanations of equivalent distance or weight measurements are equally helpful, but again optional.

Essential

What is not optional, but essential are notes that provide any alternative or a literal rendering of a text. If the Scripture is God breathed then any uncertainty as to the meaning in translation of a passage requires the translator to add notes so the onus on understanding then is passed over to the reader. At the very least this helps prevent the misuse of a passage as a proof text when a note demonstrates otherwise.

The following chapters in this section therefore provide evidence to assist understanding of passages that have missed out on having notes. Some like Genesis 2:17, Psalm 139:16 and 1 Corinthians 14:34 have had these notes in some versions, but their absence elsewhere has been seen to cause misuse, confusion and uncertainty.

17

GENESIS 2:17

This passage is used as one of the fundamental texts to a doctrine that began to take effect in the church in the 5th century. This is the doctrine that "free will is not": man is unable to choose to do good as he is dead spiritually inside and his "fallen" state inherited from birth is what limits what free will he has: his free will is bound to his fallen nature. This was the beginning of the unconditional predestination dogma in the history of church doctrine. It is assumed that the emphasis of death in Genesis 2:17 is simple and absolute and this is thereby used as a foundation to this theology.

> And the LORD God commanded the man, saying, "Of every tree of the garden you may freely eat; but of the tree of the knowledge of good and evil you shall not eat, for in the day that you eat of it you[1] shall surely die." *Genesis 2:16-17*

Here is Young:

> and of the tree of knowledge of good and evil, thou dost not eat of it, for in the day of thine eating of it – dying thou dost die.' *Genesis 2:17 Young*

Here is the note that is added to the NKJV above for the [1]:

[1] Lit. *dying you shall die*

Other versions have the same as a note. Here is the one from one of my KJVs:

Heb. *Dying thou shalt die.*

This note is important in the world of doctrine and theology as any version that omits this in this verse whilst purporting to be an accurate or good translation, as opposed to a paraphrase, is guilty of misleading the reader. It would be better to translate the whole fully.

If man in eating the fruit of the tree died completely, then without new assistance from God no man henceforth born of Adam is able spiritually at all. But the literal Hebrew is clear that a process of dying is involved and not the complete event of death. A paraphrase therefore that gives the idea that the death is immediate or complete is equally misleading. Here is the bad example of *The Message* bible:

> The moment you eat from that tree, you're dead.
> *Genesis 2:17 The Message*

Not exactly an accurate rendition of a *process* of dying, is it?

It may be the warning wanted to be conveyed by the translator more than the exact meaning of what would happen. It serves well in that emphasis. But without a note a paraphrase with the intent on assisting truth for doctrine may prefer something like this:

> The moment you eat from that tree, you're going to experience death.　　　　　*Genesis 2:17 JM*

Or perhaps,

> The moment you eat from that tree, you're going to lose life.　　　　　*Genesis 2:17 JM*

For the other versions where expansion of meaning is limited then a note is recommended.

Lit. Heb. *dying you shall die*

18

GENESIS 3:16

This is another passage that would benefit from a note being added. The main deal here is that the early church tended to use the Greek version of the Old Testament to teach from. This is known as the Septuagint and I discuss this version in the introductory chapter entitled *Incorrect Word Meaning*. In the 5th century Jerome was the man given the job of producing a new translation into the Latin of his day for the whole bible. He began to translate the Old Testament from the Septuagint, but as he compared what he did to the original Hebrew text, he then realised that the Septuagint was not as accurate a translation as it could have been. This led him to decide to translate the Old Testament for his Latin version directly from the Hebrew. This was a good thing for the God breathed Scripture is in the original and this direct translation from the Hebrew for the Old Testament has been the regular practise of translators since. However, there are exceptions to this being a good thing. If Paul, for example, who taught and quoted from the Septuagint depended on the reader's recognition that the passage in his mind was that from the Septuagint, then if the Hebrew does not convey what he was referring to, then it is needful to make a note in the appropriate passage. This is the case for Genesis 3:16. Here is the NKJV translation of the Hebrew.

> To the woman He said: "I will greatly multiply your sorrow and your conception; in pain you shall bring forth children; your desire *shall be* [1]for your husband, and he shall rule over you." *Genesis 3:16*
>
> [1] Lit. *toward*

The last section of the verse is what we need to concentrate on. But, here is Young for the whole:

> Unto the woman He said, 'Multiplying I multiply thy sorrow and thy conception, in sorrow dost thou bear children, and toward thy husband *is* thy desire, and he doth rule over thee.' *Genesis 3:16 Young*

It is of note that Young has added "*is*" as it appears to be how he read it, but faithful to his literal rule he shows this is added on his part, as did the NKJV by placing "shall be" in italics. I explain in my book *Leadership is male?* That the desire in view is in fact any new desire that overwhelms the woman as did the desire for the fruit which deceived her. God is saying to her to submit this new desire for her husband to rule over: Thus affording protection from future deception. The whole issue of deception and how it differs between men and women is in Paul's mind as he instructs the church through his writing to Timothy and the Corinthians. See the separate chapters on 1 Corinthians 11:3, 1 Timothy 2:12 and 1 Corinthian 14:34.

There is a note to one of my KJV bibles on Genesis 3:16.

> Unto the woman he said, I will greatly multiply thy sorrow and thy conception; in sorrow thou shalt bring forth children; and thy desire *shall be* [1]to thy husband, and he shall rule over thee.
>
> *Genesis 3:16 KJV*

[1] Or, *subject to thy husband.*

This would make the verse read "thy desire subject to thy husband, and he shall rule over thee" which does two things. First it dispenses with the added words and secondly, it makes sense within the understanding shared above.

Genesis 3:16 in the Septuagint (3:17 in the LXX)

> *Kai pros ton andra sou hé apostrophé sou. Kai autos sou kurieusei*   *Genesis 3:16 b*

> and thy submission* shall be to thy husband, and he shall rule over thee   *(*Gk. Turning)*

Or,

> and to your husband shall be your turning and he
> will rule over you

The literal rendering of the Hebrew is "unto your man your desire and he to rule over you". As we see above this is understood as "For your husband" in the NKJV. Young's literal is closer "and toward thy husband *is* thy desire, and he doth rule over thee." We see the "desire" is missing in the LXX, but the "turning" is clear: the submission which Paul mentions in 1 Corinthians 14:34 (see separate chapter).

So that a helpful paraphrase for Genesis 3:16 in the light of the above which would be good to see is something like:

> . . . submit your desire to your husband as he is to
> rule over you about it.   *Genesis 3:16 JM*

Thus giving a fuller appreciation of what is in view for the reader. For the more literal versions a note like this would help:

> Septuagint: your submission shall be to your
> husband (Gk. Lit. your turning). See 1 Cor.14:34

19

PSALM 139:16

The importance of notes in bible translations can be well seen in a passage like Psalm 139. Here is the affected portion:

> For You have formed my inward parts; You have covered me in my mother's womb. I will praise You, for I am fearfully *and* wonderfully made; marvelous are Your works, and *that* my soul knows very well. My frame was not hidden from You, when I was made in secret, *and* skillfully wrought in the lowest parts of the earth. Your eyes saw my substance, being yet unformed. And in Your book they all were written, the days fashioned for me, when *as yet there were* none of them.   *Psalm 139:13-16*

This passage especially in the NIV can be seen as useful to the doctrine of unconditional predestination that began in the 5th century,

> Your eyes saw my unformed body; all the days ordained for me were written in your book before one of them came to be.   *Psalm 139:16 NIV*

If God has planned all the days of our lives before they existed, then unconditional predestination is given a proof text in this passage translated in this manner. This meaning is equally to be seen in other paraphrase versions like the New Living Translation.

> You saw me before I was born. Every day of my life was recorded in your book. Every moment was laid out before a single day had passed.   *Psalm 139:16 NLT*

When I first looked at this passage I practised what I had regular recourse to doing up to then. I looked the text up in all the versions of the bible I had copies of. Nowadays it is so much faster and helpful to go online and go from one version to another to see, but there – where notes are not always present – would be missed what I read in a note in the margin of one of my KJV bibles: I will quote the text and then the notes.

> Thine eyes did see my substance, yet being unperfect; and in thy book [1]all *my members* were written, [2]*which* in continuance were fashioned, when *as yet there was* none of them.   *Psalm 139:16 KJV*
>
> [1] Heb. *all of them*.
> [2] Or, what *days they should be fashioned*.

What this direct translation gives us and assists with the notes is that: The days that various parts of the body of the baby were to be formed in the womb were recorded is in view. This is a world apart in meaning from the days of the life of the person after they are born being recorded. And the idea that "the days of one's life beyond birth" is being mentioned is out of context. The context and overall observation in the passage is about what is going in the womb. Here is Young's translation:

> Mine unformed substance Thine eyes saw, And on Thy book all of them are written, The days they were formed – And not one among them.
>
> *Psalm 139:16 Young*

So a note in translation is of vital importance to retain or add if the translation is not to be misused: Unless it is more accurately put, as per Young's example.

20

JOHN 1:12 ET AL

Translation of a word or phrase is easy when the meaning of the word or phrase is understood. However the bane or indeed the dismay of many a live translator is the need to translate a joke or a gem of wisdom where there are no equal parallel in the tongue to be translated into. Such that "Cat's eyes" in the middle of the road referring to the two circular reflectors in the middle of English roads if unknown by the translator would be turned into "eyes of cats" or stumped and, if known, perhaps just as "The reflectors for headlights embedded in the middle of roads". It is worth repeating that translation is not just about a word's meaning and the grammar involved, but also what is meant by the use of a particular set of words when used together. Just as I explained in the earlier chapter *Three measures of meal* the need to understand what is meant is more important so mistranslation does not occur and the need thereby to translate the word "three" was made clear.

So, "cat's eyes" in another language if translated "the eyes of cats" are best translated with a note added: "NOTE – the 2 round car headlight reflectors in the middle of country roads in the UK look like a small animal and have been nicknamed "cat's eyes". Here in the importance of notes section I wish to highlight the need to explain the meaning of the phrase "believing in the name" with the use of a simple note.

> But as many as received Him, to them He gave the right to become children of God, *even* to those who believe in His name.   *John 1:12*

This is the first time John is recorded in the normal New Testament order to use this favourite phrase of his. I say in the normal New Testament order as John's gospel and his letters may have been written last of the New Testament books and the common order is to have the gospels as the first four books of the New Testament.

There are several more times "believing in the name" is used and significant among them is John 3:18, which will lead on to my method of explaining what I believe is meant by this phrase. As the title of this chapter indicates by "et al" meaning "and others", John 1:12 is joined by more places where John uses the phrase.

> He who believes in Him is not condemned; but he who does not believe is condemned already, because he has not believed in the name of the only begotten Son of God.   *John 3:18*

Now the common reading of "believing in the name" is to see this as a reference to the title and very own first name of the Lord: "Jesus". This indeed was how I read it for many years from the time I became a Christian and onwards for about 21 years. Until, I came to learn and begin to understand what I have perhaps best explained since in what I have titled *The Meaning of Born Again* which is now the title of a chapter in my book *Will there be Non-Christians in heaven?*

The good thing of having it as a chapter in that book is that it helps to provide understanding within the ongoing chapters explaining the need for evangelism and also, in another chapter entitled *The Wicked* the giving of recognition that universalism – the idea that all will eventually be saved – is indeed false with a clear section on hell's reality. Here in this book, the purpose is to show there is a need for a note; not to explain all the way how this understanding fits in with everything else. So *The meaning of born again* here is an adapted version of that chapter.

The meaning of born again

The Meaning of Born Again explains from the Bible how the experience called "rebirth" realistically is not just about those really known as Christians, but about all those who hunger and thirst for righteousness (Matthew 5:6) and as such practise it (1 John 2:29) and yet are not - yet or ever - known as Christians.

The phrase "born again" was first used by Jesus during a conversation with a Pharisee named Nicodemus. The event is recorded for us in John 3.

The predominant view of this phrase is that it involves the act of becoming a Christian. It is for this reason that evangelists have often been heard to say "Have you been born again?"

Whilst this is the generally accepted view, I believe – and aim to demonstrate – that it is indeed an event which occurs to some Christians at conversion, but that it is equally or more often experienced by many non-Christians whether they go on to become Christians or not. The reason that this has been viewed as related to the act of becoming a Christian is that in John chapter 3, verses 15, 16 and 18 mention is made of "belief in Him". This is preceded in verse 14 with Jesus mentioning that "**the Son of Man**" must be lifted up. Since the whole paragraph includes mention of "born again" and belief in the Son of Man, it is easy to think that both are connected. Since the Son of Man is Jesus himself, it would be natural to understand this belief to just mean the act of becoming a Christian.

However, this is a retrospective understanding, because when Jesus was talking with Nicodemus, there were no Christians per se, just Jews and Gentiles. Jesus had not yet died and risen from the dead, and the Church was not yet a reality. Furthermore, Jesus makes a clarification of what he means by "belief in him" in verse 18 which qualifies all the previous references to this in the passage.

By "qualify" I mean it is explicit that belief in him is fully restricted to the meaning given in the qualification. This is what he said:

> He who believes in Him is not condemned; but he
> who does not believe is condemned already, because
> he has not believed in the name of the only begotten
> Son of God.   *John 3:18*

This verse is then immediately reinforced by the next which starts by saying: "**And this is the condemnation . . .**" In other words Jesus immediately expands on his discourse about condemnation and the necessary belief by clarifying further what it involves.

Bearing this in mind and going on to include this next verse, let us see what believing in "**the name of the only begotten Son of God**" means. In John 3:18 Jesus is saying that belief in Him involves belief in "**the name . . .**" He is not saying: Believe in my title name "Jesus", but something which was understood by the Greek speaker of the day. I believe this phrase belief in "**the name**" involves belief in the character, or attributes of the person concerned, and does not require a conscious awareness of the person himself, but the facets of their personality only, i.e. their character. It is not their title or known forename or surname, but their character which is represented by the phrase "the name".

The *Onoma* Enigma

The Greek word for name is *onoma* and there is indeed an enigma or difficulty in understanding it. This can be seen in that it is used in several Bible passages as a reference other than to a specific name of someone or something. Indeed, there are various places where it does not refer to someone's particular autograph – but there are many where it does – hence the difficulty. Such a case in point may be seen in Matthew 18:15-20, which ends with:

> For where two or three are gathered together in My name, I am there in the midst of them.
>
> *Matthew 18:20*

Jesus' meaning here is other than to his own particular title. This is perhaps best seen in the following passage where Jesus is praying:

> I have manifested Your name to the men whom You have given Me out of the world . . . Holy Father, keep through Your name those whom You have given Me, that they may be one as We *are*. While I was with them in the world, I kept them in Your name . . . And I have declared to them Your name, and will declare *it*, that the love with which You loved Me may be in them, and I in them.   *John 17:6, 11-12, 26*

It can be seen Jesus is not talking about the Father's title – his particular name. If he were, verse 26 would be nonsense:

> And I have declared to them Your name, and will declare . . .
>
> *John 17:26a*

In other words, if this was a particular title belonging to the Father which Jesus says he had made known, then it does not make sense that he should say he will make them know it further, a second time – especially when the second half of the sentence is included:

> . . . that the love with which You loved Me may be in them, and I in them. *John 17:26b*

It means in order that the Father's love and Jesus' presence may be in his disciples, this facet, or faculty, as understood by the Father's "**name**" needs to be continuously made known or appreciated. He is saying that this ongoing declaration is what enables the love of the Father and the presence of Jesus to be in the disciples.

So what does *onoma* mean in such cases?

To help us, we will look at a few more occurrences in Scripture so the essence of the meaning can be further grasped.

> a) [Jesus is] . . . far above all principality and power and might and dominion, and every name that is named, not only in this age but also in that which is to come. *Ephesians 1:21*

Here "name" (translated from *onomatos*) the emphasis is on an authority, a position of importance. Not unlike the English use of the word when one says "He has made a bit of a name for himself".

> b) [Jesus] . . . has by inheritance obtained a more
> excellent name than they [angels].   *Hebrews 1:4*

Here, the meaning is more in the nature of a report; a
standing; a reputation. In general, someone's particular
name represents or implies a certain authority, character,
rank, power, majesty, excellence. In the New Testament
Greek, the use of *onoma* shows that in itself it is
synonymous with these attributes. In Greek use therefore, it can be seen that what is expressed more directly
by the word "name" itself, in English is only implied.
Referring back to our example of Matthew:

> For where two or three are gathered together in My
> name, I am there in the midst of them.
> *Matthew 18:20*

The emphasis is on a gathering with the attitudes
and frame of mind of Jesus – the attributes of Jesus'
character. He said that he did not seek his own glory
(John 8:50); always did those things that pleased the
Father (John 8:29); he spoke the truth which he
heard from God (John 8:40); etcetera. With these
facets of attitude clearly in place, not only is Jesus
in the midst of the gathering, but prayers made
there will be answered, and decisions made will have
heaven's full backing, for that is the context of Matthew
18:15-20.

The synonymous understanding of *onoma* in
the preceding John 17 passage has to do with the

character and attributes of the Father. So that when Jesus says he has revealed His name (the Father's) to his disciples, he is referring to the ways and manners of the Father – the character, traits and qualities. When he says he has kept them in the Father's name, he is saying . . . in the understanding of the grace and truth of the character of God – such that proper discerning and protection is obtained in being able to see the false and the wrong by the witness of the true and real: When he says he will make known the name, he is saying that he will make them aware of these understandings in practise. With this meaning we can have a better view of:

> And I have declared to them Your name, and will declare *it*, that the love with which You loved Me may be in them, and I in them.   *John 17:26*

A full appreciation of God's heart and attitudes enables His love and Jesus' presence to be manifest.

Believing in the Name of the Son of God

With the preceding observations in mind passages referring to a belief in "the name of the Son of God" can be viewed in a way different from the current trend. John, the writer of the gospel, also wrote a number of letters. On a par with his usage of the word *onoma* in John 17 we find this passage at the end of his first letter:

These things I have written to you who believe in the name of the Son of God, that you may know that you have eternal life, *and that you may *continue to* believe in the name of the Son of God.

1 John 5:13

*The Nestle – Aland Greek New Testament Text in the 26th Edition, and the United Bible Societies Greek New Testament Text in the 3rd Edition omit the rest of this verse – The Greek Text from which some bible versions are translated. The Majority Text (a close consensus of the majority of Greek manuscripts) and the "Received Text" which is what the KJV, NKJV and Young translate from include it and are in line with John's use of the phrase in his gospel.

Notice also that the words "*continue to*" are in italics which is a common practise to signify that these words were added by the translator. Young's Literal translation of this passage reads:

These things I did write to you who are believing in the name of the Son of God, that ye may know that life ye have age-during, and that ye may believe in the name of the Son of God.   *1 John 5:13 Young*

Here again we see John re-emphasising the possibility of believing in more than just a "title" by saying to those who already believe in "**the name**", that his instructions in writing would help them comprehend more fully "**the name**" of the Son of God. It kind of parallels Jesus' own use of the phrase in John 17. The invisible attributes and character "**of the Son of God**" would be better understood as a result of what John had just written. He started the letter by writing: "**God is light and in Him is no darkness at all**" (1 John 1:5). He went on to apply this by writing: "**He who says he is in the light, and hates his brother, is in darkness until now.**" (1 John 2:9). This also involves not loving the world, which is synonymous with "**. . . the lust of the flesh, the lust of the eyes, and the pride of life**" (1 John 2:15-16). He then explains how to recognise deception: "**If you know that He is righteous, you know that everyone who practises righteousness is born of Him . . . let no one deceive you. He who practises righteousness is righteous, just as He is righteous**" (1 John 2:29, 3:7). He expanded further on this and then returned to "**. . . let us love one another, for love is of God; and everyone who loves is born of God and knows God. He who does not love does not know God, for God is love.**" (1 John 4:7-8). John finishes the letter with: "**. . . these things I have written . . . that you may know . . . and that you may *continue to* believe in the name of the Son of God.**" (1 John 5:13). The whole letter is full of references to the character and attributes of God and how to recognise them in others. The letter also contrasts these to that of the enemy's attributes. This further attests to the "belief in the name of the Son of God" having nothing to do with believing the first name of our Lord: "Jesus" or any "tag-word" or "title" of the Son of God, but instead his attributes and character.

John Three and the Light

Though it may be thought that the "belief in the name" is now understood sufficiently as belief in the character traits of the person involved without knowing the person by means of the preceding section, it is needful to reinforce this in the context in which it is used in John 3 so this ongoing section of the borrowed chapter is also included.

In John 3 Jesus specifies clearly what one needs to believe in to attain everlasting life. The fact that he does this by saying: **"He who believes in Him is not condemned; but he who does not believe is condemned already"** (John 3:18) in terms of **"because he has not believed in *the name* of the only begotten Son of God."** (*italics* mine), shows that an understanding from Scripture itself of "believing in *the name*" is crucial – as just explained – before attempting to digest the whole passage of John 3:1-21. Let us now look at the verses in question to see if the understanding gleaned through the preceding deliberations agrees. As we have already stated Jesus expands upon the condemnation referred to in John 3:18 – he says:

> And this is the condemnation, that the light has come into the world, and men loved darkness rather than light, because their deeds were evil. *John 3:19*

Jesus is saying that light of some kind has been observed, but rejected in favour of darkness, by those who are then condemned by that very rejection. This is in line with not believing in "**the name**" because it is an extension of the previous verse which says that a person is condemned already "**because he has not believed in *the name* of the only begotten Son of God**". We know that this is an extension of the earlier statement because Jesus then said: "**And *this* is the condemnation . . .**" (*italics* mine in both preceding quotes).

So those who reject the light but love darkness instead, are those who do not believe, in "**the name**" – the two states are synonymous with each other. All those in this state of loving darkness show this is so in their lives "**because their deeds were evil**". We read in verse 20:

> For everyone practising evil hates the light and does not come to the light, lest his deeds should be exposed. *John 3:20*

Everyone who loves darkness is involved in practising evil; he does not love what is right and his deeds are wicked: wholly selfish, a liar, lover of pleasure rather than others, proud of himself, etc. But, where does this light come from? In John, we read earlier about Jesus as the Logos, the Word, and his activity as the:

> . . . Light which gives light to every man who comes
> into the world. *John 1:9*

Indeed, Verse 4 tells us:

> In Him was life, and the life was the light of men.
> *John 1:4*

Both these verses tell us that everyone has an opportunity where the spiritual light shines in their life, contrasting with the darkness. John writes on, that as the light of the world (also known as "**the light of life**" cf. John 8:12 and Job 33:30) Jesus, the Logos, was in the world and although the world was made through him, it did not [want to] know him (John 1:10). In Verse 11 we read that he also came to his own, but his own did not receive him either. This is also mentioned by Paul, where he refers to the people of Israel, God's chosen (see Ezekiel 20:5) as rebellious: As a warning to Christians in 1 Corinthians 10:9 Paul says: "**. . . nor let us tempt Christ, as some of them also tempted, and were destroyed by serpents**" (see Numbers 21:5-6). Paul was aware that Christ had not been received in general by "his own" – the people of Israel.

But there is good news, for John goes on to write (John 1:12): "**. . . as many as received Him**", – that is to say, referring to verses 10 and 11, as many in the world and of his own (the people of Israel) who received Him – note the clear cause and effect here – "**. . . He gave the right to become children of God, *even* to those who believe in His name**". Here then is a sense in which we have come full circle, because this also identifies receiving the light as synonymous with "**believing in His name**".

Notice in John 1 that this is mentioned before "the Word – the Logos" is told us as becoming flesh (God incarnate), which is not written about until verse 14. Receiving the light, which is the same as believing in "**the name**" was therefore an experience possible for anyone on earth before Jesus was born. Since Jesus is also "**the same yesterday, today and forever**" (Hebrews 13:8), and the fact that by his Spirit he continues to be omnipresent – as testified by his promise "**I am with you always**" (Matthew 28:20) – then this is also an experience possible for anyone on earth today. This is why I believe that it is the same experience as being "**born again**".

The "receiving of him" also mentioned as "believing in His name" (John 1:12), is as John also writes in 3:20 a "coming to the light". It is a receiving of the Spirit of Christ by "belief in the name". It is therefore easy with that appreciation to then understand that turning one's back on the light, indicates a life of evil deeds, for Paul also wrote:

> So then, those who are in the flesh cannot please God. But you are not in the flesh but in the Spirit, if indeed the Spirit of God dwells in you. Now if anyone does not have the Spirit of Christ, he is not His.
>
> *Romans 8:8-9*

Those who come to the light are those who receive the Spirit of Christ and as the last verse in the John 3:1-21 passage tells us:

> But he who does the truth comes to the light, that his deeds may be clearly seen, that they have been done in God.
>
> *John 3:21*

This corresponds to John's first letter mentioned earlier, where he writes:

> In this the children of God and the children of the devil are manifest: Whoever does not practise righteousness is not of God, nor *is* he who does not love his brother.
>
> *1 John 3:10*

Indeed, a few verses before he says that "**everyone who practises righteousness is born of Him**", (1 John 2:29) – which is where we can now really look at what Jesus said about being "**born again**". Having expanded upon the immediate context of Jesus' discussion about being "**born again**" we can now see how it fits into the overall picture: The surroundings being visible, a clear view of "**born again**" is possible. I include this next section of the updated and adapted chapter from the title *Will there be Non-Christians in heaven?* to provide a full account of the meaning of this important phrase. I will then close with an appropriate note that should be added to the passages that contain "believing in the name".

Born Again – A commentary

John Three begins with Nicodemus, a teacher of religion, visiting Jesus by night. This was a good time to visit, because it was a private time away from the daytime crowds, but also because any religious leader unhappy about a visit to Jesus by a fellow teacher need not know about it. Nicodemus opens his discussion with Jesus by expressing his reason for believing that Jesus is a man of God – hence his desire to talk with him. Jesus makes use of the occasion to express a fundamental spiritual truth:

> Most assuredly, I say to you, unless one is born again, he cannot see the kingdom of God. *John 3:3*

The Greek word for "again" here is *anóthen*. It is also translated "from above" in John 3:31; James 1:17; 3:15, etc. Sometimes it is "from the first", e.g. Luke 1:3 and Acts 26:5; Also, "top" in Matthew 27:51; Mark 15:38 and John 19:23. The word is translated "anew" in Galatians 4:9, and this emphasis of a new or second time: "again" is what is clearly understood in John 3:3 and 3:7, as shown by Nicodemus' immediate reply "**How . . . born . . . a second time?**" (John 3:4).

What Jesus was effectively saying, was that you must be born a second time before you can see the kingdom of God – this was certainly how Nicodemus understood what was said:

> How can a man be born when he is old? Can he
> enter a second time into his mother's womb and be
> born? *John 3:4*

So confirming the concept that this truth involved
a second birthing, but expanding on the meaning of
this second birth, Jesus went on to say:

> Most assuredly, I say to you, unless one is born of
> water and the Spirit, he cannot enter the kingdom
> of God. *John 3:5*

Jesus, by saying "**born of water *and* the Spirit**"
(italics mine), tells us that there are two births: one
is of water and one is of the Spirit. Without both, a
person cannot enter the kingdom of God. The birth
of water is the first birth and is the experience of
everyone alive. It is the birth Nicodemus visualised
with his response, i.e. born out of the waters of the
womb in which he was formed. The literal Greek
is "born – that is, begotten, birthed, made up, or
manufactured – out of water and spirit". The definite
article "the" is not there preceding "spirit". But there
is the Greek word *ek* which means "from" or "out
of" and shows the emphasis is "out of which one is
birthed". The birth of the Spirit (literally – out of
spirit) is the second birth, and is a very different kind
of birth to the first. To give more emphasis, Jesus
immediately clarifies this point:

> That which is born of the flesh is flesh, and that
> which is born of the Spirit is spirit.   *John 3:6*

In other words the first birth – that of water – is the
birth of the flesh.

By contrast, the second birth is a spiritual event,
and is a prerequisite to see and enter the kingdom of
God. Jesus emphasised this when he said:

> Do not marvel that I said to you, 'You must be
> born again'.   *John 3:7*

"Must" here is from the Greek word *dei* – "it is
needful" in the sense of "ought"; "it is right (and
proper)"; "correct"; "the right (good) thing (to do)";
"incumbent"; "should"; "behoveth" – as in Mark
13:14 "**where it ought not**"; Luke 12:12; Luke
13:14, et al. This is unlike *anagké* – "compulsory",
"essential", "obligatory" – as in Romans 13:5; Luke
14:18; Jude 3; Hebrews 7:12. **It is unwise therefore,
to infer from John 3:7, that it is "essential" they
must be born again**: Jesus is not saying that *to*
Nicodemus in this verse. But he already made it
clear differently – i.e. it is "essential" to be born again
– before one can see or enter the kingdom of God, by
saying you cannot unless in John 3:3 and 3:5. This is
a truth from these verses, and can be stated from
these; it is not from John 3:7, and cannot be said
from that. Jesus saying "**You must be born again**" is

without an emphasis on Nicodemus himself being called upon to be born again. Nicodemus by coming to Jesus was already showing that he was and Jesus' purpose is to explain the need for rebirth as an understanding, a truth to be grasped. Not for Nicodemus' actual present state. The act of being born again as being explained is not a wholly conscious event and thereby this passage is not helpful to impose a meaning suggesting it is.

Jesus is not suggesting Nicodemus is not already born again, but that this is what is needed before one can see or enter the kingdom of God. He then goes on to say how this second birth reveals its occurrence:

> The wind blows where it wishes, and you hear the sound of it, but cannot tell where it comes from and where it goes. So is everyone who is born of the Spirit. *John 3:8*

Jesus is saying that although the wind exists, you can only know of its movements by the effects it creates in sound and movement, but you cannot see it come or go. This is how it is for everyone who is born of (out of) the Spirit. It is a spiritual event which you cannot understand fully – it is not a wholly conscious experience. You can only really know of its existence by its effect in and through the individual. Being born again is not therefore something that occurs out of a conscious commitment of your will and mind to God or His Son. It is not therefore the act of becoming a Christian. That is a conscious act of becoming a follower of Jesus Christ, and acknowledging Him as your Saviour and Lord. The second birth in on the other hand not a wholly conscious occurrence – the event of being born again is primarily spiritual. It occurs due to the influence of the "surrounding" Holy Spirit, not unlike being formed in our mother's womb "surrounded" by water, but not conscious of it.

For a person born again therefore assurance of eternal life (since it is not a wholly conscious event) is not available until they go on to know the promises of God's Word. These can be understood and gained after becoming a Christian, together with all the other benefits of being a full part of the Church. This is explained in the chapter on Evangelism in the afore mentioned book. So from the passage in John 3 so far we can see that being born again is not the act of becoming a Christian. By Jesus' talking of belief in him in the remaining verses, the understanding arises that rebirth and belief are linked. It is due to this the idea has arisen – I believe erroneously – that being born again is equivalent to becoming a Christian. But we saw in the preceding discussions how Jesus' own definition of what this belief in him consists of, from verse 18 onwards, it is not the same as becoming a committed Christian. We saw this because a conscious knowledge of the person believed in (i.e. Jesus by his title) was not in question, nor any knowledge about him. The issue of belief rests wholly and only on believing the attributes of that person – the righteousness they stand for, the love, the truth, etc. This was further confirmed through John 1, because the people who lived before Jesus, and could not therefore have any knowledge of him, are clearly shown as receiving him (the light). This is understood in John 1:12b as "**believe in His name**", and further confirmed in John's letter where he wrote:

> . . . everyone who practises righteousness is born of Him . . . everyone who loves is born of God and knows God.   *1 John 2:29 and 4:7*

It is incongruous to think that no one practised righteousness before Jesus came in the flesh. This agrees of course with the last verse of the John 3 passage in question:

> But he who does the truth comes to the light, that his deeds may be clearly seen, that they have been done in God.   *John 3:21*

Done in God

Therefore, those who believe in what is right – "**does the truth**" – as the verse just quoted says, are those who receive him (the light) as John writes in 1:12. Believing in these attributes of the Son of God releases God's enabling and by His Spirit (out of His Spirit) the believer becomes (is begotten) a child of God. It is due to this that the deeds they do are said to be "**done in God**". That is, the practise of righteousness (1 John 2:29) is as a result of God's working. It is therefore not surprising that Jesus said:

> Blessed *are* those who hunger and thirst for right-eousness, for they shall be filled.　　*Matthew 5:6*

John 1 makes it clear (verses 4 & 9) that the opportunity – the reality of the possibility – of "receiving him" is available universally. Everyone without exception is shown by these verses as availed by God of the opportunity to receive the light. It is also clearly implied in verse 12, that the "receiving" is able to be experienced by all. What is excluded from man's ability or working is the production by God of a "birthing" as a child of God. This is a work of God as a direct response to the desire for righteousness. This desire is synonymous with believing "in his name" (John 1:12b), which as we saw is also understood as "receiving him" (John 1:12a). As a consequence of this, which is explicit in John 1:12 as the cause and effect, God then enables the individual in question ("he gives the right" – Greek *exousian*, literally, "authority"), to become "a child of God". But this is not an authority – a right – which is left in human control; it is exercised exclusively by God. It is only God by His Spirit who does the production work, as made clear in:

> . . . who were born, not of blood, nor of the will of the
> flesh, nor of the will of man, but of God.   *John 1:13*

The idea that we are dead and unable to receive until God's touch is erroneous and I demonstrate this in the next but one chapter entitled *Journey into Light* in the book *Will there be Non-Christians in heaven?*. The word "of" in this verse is from the Greek word *ek* which means literally "out of" or "from". Thus this verse can be translated:

> . . . who were birthed, not out of bloods, nor out of a
> flesh's will, nor out of a man's will, but out of God.
> *John 1:13 JM*

God is the means whereby birthing of a child of God occurs. Just as commented on previously, human birth occurs out of the waters of the womb – which is being born of "bloods". The formation of a godly spirit in man is entirely a result of being immersed in the Holy Spirit (surrounding). The only human part is the inward – the heart of heart – desire to do what is right; believing in righteousness; believing in "the name of the Son of God". As a result of this and this only, God then births a child of God out of that individual. This is what is meant by "born again".

Nicodemus' Response

Jesus having further explained the truth about the spiritual birth being like the wind's activity where you can't tell where it comes from and where it goes and "So is everyone who is born of (out of) the Spirit", Nicodemus exclaims:

> How can these things be?   *John 3:9*

Nicodemus did not understand what Jesus was saying, and so Jesus replied:

> Are you the teacher of Israel, and do not know these
> things?   *John 3:10*

Jesus was amazed that Nicodemus did not grasp what he was telling him. His amazement was further expressed when he continued:

> Most assuredly, I say to you, We speak what We
> know and testify what We have seen, and you do not
> receive Our witness. If I have told you earthly things
> and you do not believe, how will you believe if I tell
> you heavenly things? No one has ascended to heaven
> but He who came down from heaven, *that is*, the Son
> of Man who is in heaven.   *John 3:11-13*

"Look! I am only telling you what I know and have witnessed, but you cannot take it in. If you cannot grasp the meaning of what I am telling you concerning earthly matters, how will you (go on to) understand the meanings of heavenly matters? After all, until the Son of Man, no-one has come down from heaven to talk of such" [my paraphrase]. At this point, Jesus then changes the subject and begins to talk about the Son of Man and the purposes of his coming to earth.

As we saw previously, he then includes with this, the understanding of the human participation connected with his earlier reference to being "born again".

> And as Moses lifted up the serpent in the wilderness, even so must the Son of Man be lifted up, that whoever believes in Him should not perish but have eternal life.   *John 3:14-15*

The "present-continuous" tense of the Greek – the Greek Present corresponds more closely in meaning to the English Present Continuous than to the Present Simple – so that Young has "**whoever is believing in him**" and thereby the NKJV quoted above should be read as "everyone who is believing in Him" (identical for Verses 15 and 16). This reveals more specifically what he is saying: "And it is incumbent upon the Son of Man to be lifted up, just like Moses did with the snake in the wilderness, so that whoever is believing in him may not perish but have eternal life". In other words, to ensure that those who already believe in him (as well as those who will in the future "be believing" in him) do not perish but have eternal life, the Son of Man must be lifted up (to provide the required sub-stitution sacrifice). At this point Jesus does not specify what this "believing in him" entails. He only goes as far as saying that this salvation (leading to eternal life) applies to those who are already in the process of believing. He goes on to say this emphatically:

> For God so loved the world that He gave His only begotten Son, that whoever believes in Him should not perish but have everlasting life. For God did not send His Son into the world to condemn the world, but that the world through Him might be saved.
>
> *John 3:16-17*

Due to the preceding verses, the emphasis here is placed on the purpose of the work of the Son of Man. Thus this classic passage can be read:

> Because God so loved the world, in order that whoever is believing in him may not perish but have everlasting life, he gave his only begotten Son.
>
> *John 3:16 JM*

> Because of this, God did not send his Son to condemn the world but that it may be saved through him. *Paraphrase of John 3:17 JM*

It is following this that Jesus then makes clear what this specific "belief in him" is all about. Verses 18-21, the last verses in this whole context of "born again" have already clarified for us above what this entails on our part. So, what was the gospel first taught by the disciples?

Jesus' Gospel

Having spent some time keeping company with and teaching his disciples, we read in Luke 9 how Jesus then sent them out to preach the kingdom of God, and to heal the sick (Luke 9:2).

> So they departed and went through the towns, preaching the gospel and healing everywhere.
>
> *Luke 9:6*

The question then arises – What was this gospel?

At this time it is evident that the disciples did not understand that Jesus would die for the sins of the world, and that he would then rise again. Indeed, Jesus later mentioned these things to come, but they could not take it in: **"They understood none of these things; this saying was hidden from them, and they did not know the things which were spoken"** (Luke 18:31-34). So the gospel which the disciples were preaching earlier had nothing to do with the "traditional gospel" as related by many Christians. Jesus' commandment to the disciples to teach the nations (Matthew 28:19) did not include this "traditional gospel" either, but only what he had commanded them – and what was this? What did the disciples know as "the gospel" when they were sent out? It would have been nothing more than the teachings of the Sermon on the Mount, the parables, and the other truths that Jesus taught and demonstrated about the kingdom of God. It did not particularly involve any other doctrine or tradition. But it did encompass how to treat your fellow man and how to love – truly from the heart – and how to love and live for God. They were teachings which enlightened the mind on the ways and attributes of God – which is why Jesus had said during his Sermon on the Mount:

> Be ye therefore perfect, even as your Father which is
> in heaven is perfect.   *Matthew 5:48 KJV*

Is it any wonder then, that throughout the pages of the gospels, we find Jesus calling on his listeners to stop doing evil deeds and to be pure minded. Nothing of wickedness or unrighteousness had any part in his character. Deliberately allowing these in one's life is active unbelief "**in the name of the only begotten Son of God**" . . . loving of "**darkness rather than light, because their deeds were evil**". Conversely, a desire for what is right is real faith "**in the name of the only begotten Son of God**" and shows them as someone who "**does the truth**"; someone who comes "**to the light**" and is not afraid, that "**his deeds may be clearly seen**" for "**they have been done in God**" (John 3:18-21). That is a person who is born again:

> If you know that He is righteous, you know that
> everyone who practises righteousness is born of Him.
>   *1 John 2:29*

In Summary

John 1:12 and 13

"Believing in His name" is believing in the attributes of God's character and anyone who does this is receiving Him: "**as many as received Him**" is those who "**believe in His name**" (John 1:12).

This facilitates God to form the spirit within man as Zechariah 12:1 states for He is the One who "**forms the spirit of man within him**" thus all of the production of that new birth is God's doing as per John 1:13 – "**who – not of blood nor of a will of flesh, nor of a will of man but – of God were begotten**" (Young). A spirit is alive and present in everyone (Ecclesiastes 12:7), but embryonic and does not go on to be fully formed for birthing without the decisions that relate to sowing to the Spirit (Galatians 6:8). This is a clear cause and effect situation: namely "**as many as received Him, to them He gave the right to become children of God**": where the cause "receiving him" has the effect of God "giving the right – the authority – to become children of God" these two verses which contain the first reference to a birthing in John's gospel is the context of the mention of the rebirth – being born again – in John 3.

Suggested Note for John 1:12 et al

All other mentions of "believing in His name" or "believing in the name of the Son of God" then also need a note referring back to John 1:12 which has this note as the 1st mention of the phrase. Namely all the passages following need a reference back to John 1:12 with the note added:

John 2:23, John 3:18, 1 John 3:23 and 1 John 5:13

> But as many as received Him, to them He gave the right to become children of God, to those who believe in His name[1].   *John 1:12*

[1] *believing in His name* – a phrase regularly used by John with the synonymous meaning of believing in the character attributes of the person mentioned.

21

ACTS 4:12

"The Bible says…" then follows the quote:

> … by the name of Jesus Christ of Nazareth … there is no other name under heaven given among men by which we must be saved. *Acts 4:10-12*

This passage is perhaps one of the most concise to point to Jesus as the one name from whom to obtain salvation. Why is it here, in a book about mistranslations?

Answer: only for one thing, it is better translated as,

> … there is no other name under heaven given among men by which we can be saved. *Acts 4:12 JM*

The word "must" is not to be understood as "compulsory": a means by which no knowledge of Jesus automatically means that no salvation is possible for that person.

Tell that to the man born deaf and blind!

No, the Greek word *dei* from which "must" is translated here is more about "it is incumbent", "it is needful", "the thing which ought to be done" rather than being about "the obligatory action or else!"

The Greek word for which "must" is compulsory, obligatory is *anagké*. This is well seen in the word translated as "must" in Paul's instruction to obey the law of the land:

> Therefore *you* must be subject, not only because of wrath but also for conscience' sake.   *Romans 13:5*

Rather than give an exhaustive look at *dei* – but also note the information on this in the preceding chapter – I will give just a few examples of its use as an indication of things which are needful, helpful, the right thing to do, in contrast in meaning to the example for *anagké* just given: obligatory and compulsory.

> Woe to you, scribes and Pharisees, hypocrites! For you pay tithe of mint and anise and cummin, and have neglected the weightier *matters* of the law: justice and mercy and faith. These you ought to have done, without leaving the others undone.
> *Matthew 23:23*

Edei here translated as "you ought".

> "But when you see the *'abomination of desolation,'* spoken of by Daniel the prophet, standing where it ought not" (let the reader understand), "then let those who are in Judea flee to the mountains."
> *Mark 13:14*

Again "ought" here is translated from *dei* as it is in the next passage.

> Therefore, since all these things will be dissolved, what manner of *persons* ought you to be in holy conduct and godliness   *2 Peter 3:11*

We can see then that the old English "it behoves", like the more modern "should" is readily translated from *edei* as per the following example.

> Should you not also have had compassion on your fellow servant, just as I had pity on you?
> *Matthew 18:33*

So if a paraphrase or more accurate rendering of Acts 4:12 is not to be given, then a note to prevent misuse as a proof text is needful.

> . . . there is no other name under heaven given among men by which we [1]must be saved.   *Acts 4:12*

> [1] *Must* is from the Greek *dei*: should, ought, it is needful

But, as mentioned a more accurate rendering for the sake of the understanding would be,

> . . . there is no other name under heaven given among men by which we can be saved.   *Acts 4:12*

22

1 CORINTHIANS 14:34

Since this passage in Corinthians is parallel in relevance to 1 Timothy 2:11-12 and both refer to Genesis 3:16 as explained in both preceding chapters this brief one is to highlight the equal need for a note to be added.

> Let your women keep silent in the churches, for they are not permitted to speak; but *they are* to be submissive, as the law also says. *1 Corinthians 14:34*

In the light of the translation of 1 Timothy 2:12 explained in the earlier chapter another passage that also needs attention is Genesis 3:16 (G3:16). For that I included a chapter in the *Use of notes* section rather than assert a new translation as being absolutely essential.

Along with the parallel passage of 1 Timothy 2:11-12 we find in 1 Corinthians 14:34 another reference to G3:16. In Timothy the reference to it is the "authority of a husband" – translation as per the chapter – and, in 1 Corinthians 14:34 it is that women are "to be submissive, as the law also says." In the book *Leadership is male?* I explain why G3:16 is the passage in view here: It is G3:16 that tells us about the husband's authority to decide over the woman who is submitting what she desires so that she need not act again on something she is deceived by her immediate reaction involving her strong desire. Her ongoing protection was provided in God's instruction to her in G3:16. This can more readily be read in the passage of G3:16 when we look at the Septuagint (LXX) version of it. Paul's regular quotes of the LXX show us that his reading of G3:16 is the passage that he had in mind and makes fuller sense of what he is talking about in Corinthians and Timothy. So that at the very least a note needs adding to the page of G3:16 in our bibles so the LXX rendering is given and at the very best the meaning out of the Hebrew with this appreciation understood needs to be given.

Too long what Paul understood by G3:16 which can be verified in his regular use of the LXX by his many quotes of that and his 2 references to this passage has been lost. Let's see it restored to full use to the benefit of all.

So that a note to be added to 1 Corinthians 14:34 is needful. However an equal note to be added to G3:16, as discussed in its own chapter, is required to be fully productive.

> Let your women keep silent in the churches, for they are not permitted to speak; but they are to be sub-missive, as the law also says[1].   *1 Corinthians 14:34*

[1] A reference to Genesis 3:16 cf. note at G3:16

23

EPHESIANS 2:8-9

An example of a passage where an added note would benefit against misuse is Ephesians 2:8-9. Although this could equally be seen as an argument to translate this altogether differently and thus assist clarification of what is meant in the Greek grammar.

> For by grace you have been saved through faith, and that not of yourselves; *it is* the gift of God, not of works, lest anyone should boast.   *Ephesians 2:8-9*

How is this misused?

In the book *So you think you're chosen?* I highlight the fact that the "free will is not" doctrine was introduced in the 5th century by Augustine. Modern adherents of that theology use this passage to "prove" that faith is a gift and not just salvation: everything mentioned in the passage in their view is the gift of God.

So if not a note, but a new translation, how could this translate to clarify the grammar?

> For by grace you have been saved through faith, and this salvation is not of yourselves, but of God the gift, not of works, lest anyone should boast.
>
> *Ephesians 2:8-9 JM*

Here we have "**And this salvation is not of yourselves, but of God the gift**" which clarifies that the gift in view is salvation and nothing else. The word "**salvation**" is not placed in italics since that is what is meant, even if the word itself is not repeated in the Greek, the very Greek grammar involved requires it to be understood that way, so whether in a paraphrase, a direct translation, or a note this truth needs to be displayed. Here is the Greek:

> *Té - gar - chariti - este - sesómenoi - dia - tés - pis-*
> *teós. * kai touto - ouk - ex - humón, * theou - to -*
> *dóron. * ouk – ex - ergón, * hina – mé – tis -*
> *kauchésétai.*   *Ephesians 2:8-9*

To help show how this literally translates here follows the two verses in full and please note that dashes are to help follow the direct translation as are the asterisks * (used here at the so-called "punctuation" breaks of the Greek Text "used" – N.B. very early extant manuscripts have no space in between words nor any punctuations):

> The – For – by/with grace – you are – saved – through – the – faith; * and this – not – out of/from – yourselves, * of God – the – gift; * not – out of/from – works, * in order that – not – anyone – to boast.   *Ephesians 2:8-9*

How can we see that a clarification is needed?

It is because ***kai touto*** translated "**and this**" is not sufficient in English alone to show what it is telling us. To understand this here is the full declension of the demonstrative pronoun *houtos* – "this"

Declension of the demonstrative *houtos* – THIS

Singular			Plural			
Male	Female	Neuter	Male	Female	Neuter	
houtos	*hauté*	***touto***	*houtoi*	*hautai*	***tauta***	- Nominative
touton	*tautén*	***touto***	*toutous*	*tautas*	***tauta***	- Accusative
toutou	*tautés*	*toutou*	*toutón*	*toutón*	*toutón*	- Genitive
toutó	*tauté*	*toutó*	*toutois*	*tautais*	*toutois*	- Dative

I have highlighted in bold the needful.

The fact that *touto* is the singular means that it refers to one thing only. So that "and this" is about a single preceding mentioned word. In this case salvation is the item in view as a gift.

A false grammatical rule

I have seen it argued that *kai touto* is a phrase used to represent all that precedes it: a reasoning based on an alleged grammatical rule that together these two words are representative of all that precede them as a phrase.

Let's not forget that grammatical rules, dictionaries and any aid to translation are after the event of the inspiration of the original text of all Scripture. This means they are subject to human error and if any pointer in the original or the recognised practise of the original authors can "speak into" an issue that assists translation then that pointer supersedes the grammatical rule or dictionary content that was put together after the original.

Why am I saying all this?

If Paul is seen to practise the use of a plural of *kai touto* and as can be seen by the declension list this would be *kai tauta*, then it follows he practised a grammatical rule that when more than one preceding word is understood by "and this" he used the plural "and these". This very simple rule then is testified to by Paul's use and speaks into Paul's use of the singular *kai touto* as referring to one thing only in Ephesians 2:8-9 i.e. salvation is the free gift in view: nothing else. Solely by the Greek grammar Paul practised.

The example I give for this practise of using *kai tauta* rather than *kai touto* to refer to more than one thing is 1 Corinthians 6:8

> No, you yourselves do wrong and defraud, AND *you do* THESE things *to your* brethren!
> *1 Corinthians 6:8 – Emphasis in CAPITALS mine*

As is the NKJV practise added words are put in italics so "and these" is not immediately seen together. Here is Young:

> but ye- ye do injustice, and ye defraud, and these-brethren!   *1 Corinthians 6:8 Young*

So let's see the original in an interlinear fashion:

> *alla*-but * *humeis*-you * *adikeite*-you do wrong *
> *kai*-and * *apostereite*-you defraud * *KAI*-AND *
> *TAUTA*-THESE * *adelphous*-brethren
>
> *1 Corinthians 6:8*

So here we see Paul using *kai tauta* the plural of *kai touto*. He uses "and these" as opposed to "and this" to say that the brethren were both doing wrong and defrauding (cheating); not just one, but both of those things. This is a clear testimony to Paul's use of *kai touto* to refer to one thing only elsewhere.

So, if fully translated:

> For by grace you have been saved through faith, and this salvation is not of yourselves, but of God the gift, not of works, lest anyone should boast.
>
> *Ephesians 2:8-9 JM*

But otherwise a note is needful to prevent misuse of the passage:

> For by grace you have been saved through faith, and that[1] not of yourselves; *it is* the gift of God, not of works, lest anyone should boast.   *Ephesians 2:8-9*

[1] "and that" in the singular refers to one preceding word: to save – salvation

FUTURE OF TRANSLATIONS

What is a fact is that languages that are in use are living and transforming constantly so that new words and new inferences on old words are continuously created and applied. Once upon a time the word "gay" was mostly about being happy, the most current use is that it is about homosexuals and the newest inference is it refers to people who are stupid or something being rubbish.

What is important is that the core truths and the accuracy of the bible text is preserved. So that it is unavoidable that new translations will continue to be needed to explain or re-phrase these truths. Two things are constantly needful: accurate knowledge of the original and new means of transmitting that into forms and language to make it accessible.

This can be achieved only by a more accurate appreciation of the grammar and the meaning of words in the original – including the meaning of the passage – as well as the regular use of notes in contemporary translations. The enemy is aware of language and the truth and will go on to deceive as to the true meaning of texts. He is into affirming false dogma with texts out of context strung together. So that all new translations need to be as up to date as possible in regards to note making so that the current proof texts of the time are either disproved or affirmed by the notes either showing a text cannot be used that way or it can.

Literal

Perhaps for the literal a cross between a bible, a book of grammar and a lexicon is needful: A few steps beyond an interlinear. Where a passage is taken apart on the same page in a flow chart or other visually helpful format to expand on the grammar of each part and meaning of each word to thereby display exactly how the translation occurs and no nuances are left out: Thus leaving all for the reader to use to the full. This would be a valuable resource for all translators and bible study.

I look forward to such a bible version coming to pass.

Paraphrase

I re-affirm my original comments at the beginning of this book that paraphrases are valuable and have an important role to play in introducing the story and sharing much of the overall text of the bible. But since the original is God breathed all paraphrases miss out on the accuracy and many truths which only a literal rendering can convey and the latter is the only source valid for doctrine so that if a paraphrase differs in meaning to a literal then the inference is not to be taught as "bible truth" but recognised and used honestly for what it is.

Paraphrases or sections of literal versions that claim to be accurate translations and are without the necessary notes to show the alternative rendering are by omission assisting the enemy in his work of deceiving the saints.

I was once asked what I thought of the *Manga bible* which is a Japanese cartoon style of depicting the events and people in the bible. The person asking was doubtful the Lord would be into such dark images to depict the text of Scripture as many passages especially in regards to the crucifixion and associated appeared that way. I had not considered the matter and decided to ask the Lord and respond with that. After all we are told,

> If any of you lacks wisdom, let him ask of God, who gives to all liberally and without reproach, and it will be given to him.   *James 1:5*

So I did, but expecting a reply, for James went on to write,

> But let him ask in faith, with no doubting, for he who doubts is like a wave of the sea driven and tossed by the wind. For let not that man suppose that he will receive anything from the Lord; *he is* a double-minded man, unstable in all his ways.
> *James 1:6-8*

What I received was a recognition that just as God had delighted in creating creatures that are bizarre and indeed frightening to some, like spiders aplenty, or the monstrous featured fish of the deep, so a seeming dark depiction is no issue, as long as it does not stray from the story it is relating. The same is true of other paraphrases. That thereby speaks into the issue of paraphrase and presentation.

Source Texts

It will be noted to the knowing reader that up till now I have made no explicit comment as to the source text for the translation of the bible: in particular the New Testament. I say explicit, for in my making the NKJV the default bible for quotes in this book and indeed my regular practise elsewhere, I am tending to affirm its stand on the original texts. The late discovery in the 19th century of two extant Greek texts as dated from the 4th century that were largely without damage caused a re-appraisal at the end of the 19th century for source material to translate the N.T. However the very unused and undamaged character of these manuscripts puts into question their reliability in their own day. In the days before printing, no true copy of Scripture was left undamaged as it was so regularly used for reading and learning. So I commend the reader to look at the introduction to the NKJV which explains well the issues of those two texts which are presently heavily used by modern versions of the bible as part of their source material for the Greek text they use to translate the New Testament. I believe that a further re-appraisal is required in that many quotes of the early Church writers which predate these two 4th century manuscripts include portions of scripture which are missing or differ from them. These quotes tend to be in the source text of the NKJV and other versions that make use of the same. To have placed so much emphasis on just two manuscripts has been unwise. It may be that not as much a majority text is required (the majority text is in itself closer to the Received Text), but what may be needful is a truer broad eclectic look at all the extant copies as well as all the early quotes from the early writers that precede these "two authorities": that is to say, quotes of the New Testament made before them which concur with other extant copies of the N.T. text then makes these other extant copies more valid as sources.

I look forward to seeing such a text being formulated.

Bible Societies

In 2001 I first produced a booklet on my initial research of the Greek word *eklektos*. I offered a 50% discount to all bible translators and several copies were purchased by the Bible Society. However to my knowledge no bibles have been produced any differently.

In 2009 I wrote a separate epilogue to my book *So you think you're chosen?* Entitled *A Message to Bible Societies*.

Here is a whole book about mistranslations. Let's see if notice will be taken.

Finally

Finally, we read,

> For the word of God *is* living and powerful, and sharper than any two-edged sword, piercing even to the division of soul and spirit, and of joints and marrow, and is a discerner of the thoughts and intents of the heart.
> *Hebrews 4:12*

I look forward to the words of the living God to be more honestly effective as such in all new translated versions of the bible. I trust this work has helped in making this possible.

In the 1980s I helped run a youth group and my regular practise was to finish any teaching time with Paul's own recommendation which I leave you with:

> Test all things; hold fast what is good.
> *1 Thessalonians 5:21*

APPENDICES

APPENDIX 1

EKLEKTOS

This Appendix serves chapter four on the word *eklektos* and chapter five. These were preceded by the introductory chapter entitled *Incorrect Word Meanings* wherein the Septuagint is shown as the version of the Old Testament quoted by Jesus and the apostles.

REFERENCE		GREEK	A DIRECT TRANSLATION	KJV (From the Hebrew)
Genesis	23:6	*tois eklektois*	our *choice* sepulchres	the *choice* of our . . .
	41:2	*eklektai*	seven cows . . . *choice* of flesh -	*fat*fleshed
	4	*tas eklektas*	*the* . . . *choice*-fleshed cows	*fat* kine
	5	*eklektoi*	seven ears . . . *choice* and good	-*rank* and good
				[rank; Eng. in the sense of complete]
				(Heb. *fat*.)
	7	*tous eklektous*	seven *choice* and full ears	- *rank* and full ears
	18	*eklektai*	*choice*-fleshed	*fat*fleshed
	20	*tas eklektas*	*choice* cows	the seven *fat* kine
Exodus	14:7	*eklektia*	six hundred *chosen* chariots	*chosen*[4] chariots
				choice chariots **NKJV**; the *best* chariots **NIV**
	30:23	*eklektēs*	the flower of *choice* myrrh	*pure* myrrh
Numbers	11:28	*ho eklektos*	Joshua . . . the *chosen* one	of his *young* men
				of his *choice* men **NKJV**;
				assistant since *youth* **NIV**
Deuteronomy	12:11	*eklekton*	every *choice* gift of yours	your *choice* vows
				(Heb. the *choice* of your vows.)

Book	Verse	Greek		
Judges	20:15	*eklektoi*	seven hundred *chosen* men of all the people	*chosen* men / **select** men NKJV; *chosen* men NIV
	34	*eklektón*	ten thousand *chosen* men out of all Israel	**select** men NKJV; *chosen* men; ***finest*** men NIV
1 Samuel (LXX: 1 Kings)	24:3	*eklektous*	three thousand men *chosen*	24:2 *chosen* men
	26:2	*eklektón*	three thousand men *chosen*	*chosen* men
2 Samuel (LXX: 2 Kings)	8:8	*tón eklektón*	the *choice* cities	N/A See note at right the LORD did ✝choose (Or, *chosen* of the LORD.)
	21:6	*eklektous*	*chosen* out for the Lord [the men]	
	22:27	*eklektou*	with the *excellent* . . .	With the **pure** . . .
	27	*eklektos*	. . . thou wilt be *excellent*	show thyself **pure**
1 Kings (LXX: 3 Kings)	3:46	*eklektoi*	ten *choice* calves	N/A
	4:23	*eklektoi*	ten *choice* calves	Ten *fat* oxen
	23	*eklektón*	and *choice* fatted does	and *fatted* fowl
2 Kings (LXX: 4 Kings)	8:12	*tous eklektous*	their *choice* men	their *young* men
	19:23	*ta eklekta*	his *choice* cypresses	the *choice* fir trees
1 Chronicles	7:40	*eklektoi*	*choice*, mighty **men**	*choice and* mighty men

It is of note that some small sections of the LXX are not found in the Hebrew scripture and therefore not in the Old Testament of our Bibles. Equally, it must be recognised that in places the translation into the Greek was 'loose' and not literal, such that when a direct counterpart in the Hebrew is non existent, the Hebrew translation into the English does not exist.

These are 2 different reasons for which N/A has been placed in the KJV column.

Reference		Greek	A Direct Translation	KJV (From the Hebrew)
	9:22	hoi eklektoi	All the *chosen* porters	*chosen* to be porters
	16:13	eklektoi	Jacob his *chosen ones*	his *±chosen ones*
	18:8	tōn eklektōn	out of *the chief* cities	N/A
Ezra	5:8	eklektois	with *choice* stones	with *great* stones
Nehemiah	5:18	eklekta	six *choice* sheep	six *choice* sheep
Job	37:11	eklekton	a cloud obscures [what is] *precious*	N/A
Psalm	17:26	eklektou	with the *excellent*	18:26 With the *pure* . . .
	26	eklektos	thou wilt be *excellent*	18:26 shew thyself *pure*
	77:31	tous eklektous	the *choice men*	78:31 the *±chosen* [men] the *choice* [men] NKJV; the *young* men NIV; (or, *young* men KJV)
	88:3	tois eklektois	my *chosen* ones	89:3 my *±chosen*
	19	eklekton	one *chosen* out of	89:19 *_chosen_ out of; one _chosen_ from NKJV; a _young man_ from NIV

	Greek		
104:6	*eklektoi*	his *chosen ones*	105:6 his †*chosen*
43	*tous eklektous*	his *chosen*	105:43 his †*chosen*
105:5	*tón eklektón*	thine *elect*	106:5 thy †*chosen*
23	*ho eklektos*	his *chosen*	106:23 his †*chosen*
140:4	*tón eklektón*	their **choice ones**	141:4 their **dainties**
Proverbs 8:19	*eklektou*	**choice** silver	**choice** silver
12:24	*eklektón*	<u>chosen men</u>	the ***diligent*** (= NKJV =NIV)
17:3	*eklektai*	**choice** hearts	N/A
Canticles 5:15	*eklektos*	**choice** as the cedars	***excellent*** as the cedars
6:8	*eklekté*	the **choice** of her	6:9 the **choice** *[one]* of her
9	*eklekté*	**choice** as the sun	6:10 ***clear*** as the sun
Isaiah 22:7	*hai eklektai*	**thy choice** valleys	***thy choicest*** valleys
8	*tous eklektous*	**the choice** houses	***the armour*** of the house
28:16	*eklektón*	a costly stone, a **choice**	a ***tried*** stone
40:30	*eklektoi*	the **choice** [men]	the ***young*** men
42:1	*ho eklektos*	Israel is my <u>chosen</u>	mine †<u>*elect*</u>
43:20	*to eklekton*	to my <u>chosen</u>	my †<u>*chosen*</u>
45:4	*tou eklektou*	Israel mine <u>*elect*</u>	Israel mine †<u>*elect*</u>

REFERENCE		GREEK	A DIRECT TRANSLATION	KJV (From the Hebrew)
	49:2	eklekton	a **choice** shaft	a **polished** shaft
	54:12	eklektous	**precious** stones	**pleasant** stones
	65:9	hoi eklektoi	mine _elect_ and my servants	mine _†elect_
	15	tois eklektois	my _chosen_	my _†chosen_
	23	hoi eklektoi	My _chosen_	65:22 mine _†elect_
Jeremiah	3:19	eklektén	a **choice** land	a **pleasant** land
				(Heb. land of desire)
	10:17	eklektois	**choice** [vessels]	the **fortress**
	22:7	tas eklektas	**thy choice** cedars	**thy choice** cedars
	26:15	ho eklektos	**thy choice** calf	46:15 **thy valiant** [men]
	31:15	eklektoi	his **choice** young men	48:15 his °_chosen_ young
				(Heb. the **choice** of. . .)
	38:39	eklektón	**choice** stones	N/A
Lamentations	1:15	eklektous	my **choice** men	my **young** men
	5:13	eklektoi	the _chosen_ men	the **young** men
	14	eklektoi	the _chosen_ men	the **young** men

Book	Ref	Greek		
Ezekiel	7:20	*eklekta*	their **choice** ornaments	the **beauty** of his ornaments
	17:22	*tón eklektón*	of the **choice** [branches] of the cedar	of the **highest** branch
	19:12	*ta eklekta*	her **choice** [branches]	her **fruit**
	14	*eklektén*	her **choice** [boughs]	her **fruit**
	25:9	*eklekten*	the **choice** land	the **glory** of the country
	27:20	*eklektón*	**choice** cattle	**precious** clothes
				(Heb. clothes of **freedom**)
	24	*eklektous*	**choice** stores	chests of **rich** apparel
	31:16	*ta eklekta*	the **choice** [plants]	the **choice** and best
Daniel	11:15	*hoi eklektoi*	his *chosen* ones	his °*chosen* people
				his **choice** troops **NKJV**; their **best** troops
				NIV; ((Heb. the people of his *choices*))
Amos	5:11	*eklekta*	**choice** gifts	**burdens** of wheat
Habbakkuk	1:16	*eklekta*	meats **choice**	meat **plenteous**
				(Or, **dainty**; Heb. **fat**)
Haggai	2:7	*ta eklekta*	the **choice** [portions] of all the nations	the **desire** of all nations
Zechariah	7:14	*eklektén*	the **choice** land	the **pleasant** land
	11:16	*tón eklektón*	the flesh of **the choice** [ones]	eat the flesh of **the fat**

Robert Young author of the Analytical Concordance to the Bible makes a valuable comment. In his research involving the useage of every word of Greek and Hebrew used in the Bible he more than most can testify to the reality of what *eklektos* stood for. In the introduction to the New Testament of his Literal Version[5] of the Bible, he has listed what should be read in place of certain words. He lists a minimum of 100 words with a return to the original intent alongside.

> For chosen he has put: read choice one,   very often in N.T.
> For elect: read choice one,   very often in S.S.

Basic analysis

There are 82 occasions where the word *eklektos* is found in the Septuagint. Of these 7 have no corresponding section of writing in the Hebrew scripture as found translated in the Old Testament. This leaves us with 75 places where the word is found.

Out of 75 places 23 have been translated from the Hebrew into the KJV as chosen (18); elect (4); choose (1).

This leaves us with 52 places where the translation (in the KJV) from the Hebrew words associated with *eklektos* are as follows:

> choice (9); young [men] (6); pure (5); fat (4); pleasant (3); rank [Eng. complete] (2); highest [branch] (1); fatted (1); great [stones] (1); diligent (1); excellent (1); clear [as the sun] (1); thy choicest [valley] (1); the armour [of the house] (1); tried [stone] (1); polished [shaft] (1); beauty (1); fruit (1); glory (1); precious [clothes] (1); rich [apparel] (1); burdens [of wheat] (1); plenteous (or, dainty) [meat] (1); the desire [of all nations] (1); valiant (1); dainties (1).

It is undisputed therefore that the Greek thinkers who put together the Septuagint saw the understanding of quality as the prominent flavour for the word *eklektos*.

As mentioned above there are however 18 places (in the KJV) where chosen is found, 3 with elect and 1 with choose from Hebrew words associated with *eklektos*. The references for these are as follows:

Chosen: Exodus 14:7**; Judges 20:15**; Judges 20:34**;
          1 Samuel 24:3; 1 Samuel 26:2; 1 Chronicles 9:22;
          1 Chronicles 16:13; Psalm 77:31**; Psalm 88:3;
          Psalm 88:19**; Psalm 104:6; Psalm 104:43; Psalm
          105:5; Psalm 105:23; Isaiah 43:20; Isaiah 65:15;
          Jeremiah 31:15**; Daniel 11:15**
Elect: Isaiah 42:1; Isaiah 45:4; Isaiah 65:9
Choose: 2 Samuel 21:6

I have marked 7 of the references with a double star because they are
translated differently in the margin of the KJV or other versions like
the NKJV or NIV as follows:

Exodus 14:7	choice chariots **NKJV**	the best chariots **NIV**
Judges 20:15	select men **NKJV**	chosen men **NIV**
Judges 20:34	select men **NKJV**	finest men **NIV**
Psalm 77:31	the choice [men] **NKJV**	the young men **NIV**
		(Or, young men **KJV**)
Psalm 88:19	one chosen from **NKJV**	a young man **NIV**
Jeremiah 31:15	**KJV** margin: Heb.	
(48:15 in our bibles)	the choice of . . .	
Daniel 11:15	his choice troops **NKJV**	their best troops **NIV**

This means that 7 can reasonably be removed from the list as
meaning chosen and added to the one where quality is the prime
emphasis. There is doubt of a 'selection' being the emphasis.

New tally: quality (type) 59; chosen 11; elect 4; choose 1

The "selection" words can be looked at with reference to the Hebrew
words from which they are translated:

          *BACHAR   chosen (2); [excellent (1)]
          †BACHIR   chosen (8); elect (4); choose (1)
          ^BARAR   chosen (1)

BACHAR

Not only is BACHAR translated as "excellent" in Song of Solomon 5:15, it is found translated in the LXX without reference to *eklektos*:

> As "young men" in 2 Samuel 6:1, 1 Kings 12:21,
> 2 Chronicles 11:1 and Jeremiah 29:19 (49:19)
> As "mighty warriors" in 2 Chronicles 13:3 and 13:17
> As "mighty men" in 2 Chronicles 13:17
> As "youths" in Jeremiah 27:44 (50:44)

This of course brings doubt on a "selection" emphasis.

New tally: quality (type) 61; chosen 9; elect 4; choose 1

BACHAR translations

However, let's take a closer look at BACHAR where it is translated as follows in the **KJV** and see the counterpart in the LXX. The following thereby identifies which Greek word was used in the LXX portion for the Hebrew word used. First comes the English word in alphabetical order as found in the KJV, then under each English word comes the Greek word in alphabetical order used to translate the Hebrew word BACHAR in the LXX. In bold are the instances where *eklektos* are found.

Acceptable
Proverbs 21:3   *arestos* - pleasing

Appoint ["commands" NKJV]
2 Samuel 15:15   *haireó* is used
Also in Job 34:4

Be rather
Psalm 84:10 (LXX83:10)   *eklegó* is used

Choice
Proverbs 8:10   *dokimadzó* (*chrusion*) – tried
                                        (gold)

2 Chronicles 25:5	*dunatos*
Proverbs 8:19	***eklektos* KJV "choice silver"**
Proverbs 10:20	*puroó (argurion)* – tried (silver)

Choose

1 Chronicles 28:4   *hairetidzó*
Also in 1 Chronicles 28:6, 28:10, 29:1; 2 Chronicles 29:11; Psalm 25:12 (LXX24:12), 119:30 (LXX118:30), 119:73 (LXX118:73); Ezekiel 20:5; Haggai 2:23; Zechariah 1:17, 2:12

Genesis 6:2   *eklegó*
Also in Genesis 13:11; Numbers 16:5, 16:7, 17:5; Deuteronomy 4:37, 7:7, 10:15, 12:5, 12:11, 12:14, 12:18, 12:21, 14:2, 14:23, 14:24, 14:25, 15:20, 16:2, 16:6, 16:7, 16:11, 16:15, 16:16, 17:8, 17:10, 17:15, 18:5, 18:6, 21:5, 26:2, 30:19, 31:11; Joshua 9:27, 24:15, 24:22; Judges 5:8, 10:14; 1 Samuel 2:28, 8:18, 10:24, 12:13, 13:2, 16:8, 16:9, 16:10, 17:40; 2 Samuel 6:21, 16:18, 24:12; 1 Kings 3:8, 8:16, 8:44, 8:48, 11:13, 11:32, 11:34, 11:36, 14:21, 18:23, 18:25; 2 Kings 21:7, 23:27; 1 Chronicles 15:2, 19:10, 21:10, 28:4, 28:5; 2 Chronicles 6:5, 6:5, 6:6, 6:6, 6:34, 6:38, 7:12, 7:16, 12:13, 33:7; Nehemiah 1:9, 9:7; Job 29:25, 34:33, 36:21; Psalm 33:12 (LXX32:12), 47:4 (LXX46:4), 65:4 (LXX64:4), 78:67 (LXX7:67), 78:68 (LXX77:68), 78:70 (LXX77:70), 105:26 (LXX104:26), 132:13 (LXX131:13), 135:4 (LXX134:4); Isaiah 7:15, 7:16, 14:1, 40:20, 41:8, 41:9, 41:24, 43:10, 44:1, 44:2, 49:7, 56:4, 58:5, 58:6, 65:12, 66:3, 66:4, 66:4; Zechariah 3:2

Exodus 17:9   *epilegó*
Also in Exodus 18:25; Joshua 8:3; 2 Samuel 10:9, 17:1

Deuteronomy 7:6   *proaireó*
Also in Proverbs 1:29

Deuteronomy 23:16 has portion of verse containing BACHAR not translated.
Also in 1 Samuel 20:30; Job 7:15, 9:14, 15:5

Proverbs 3:31 portion of verse translated differently
Also in Isaiah 1:29, 48:10

Jeremiah 33:24 Section of Jeremiah missing in LXX

Chosen

Jeremiah 8:3		*haireó*	
2 Chronicles 13:3		*anér dunatos* – mighty man	
Also in 2 Chronicles 13:17			

2 Chronicles 13:3   *dunatos* - mighty

Exodus 14:7	*eklektos*	KJV chosen	NKJV choice	NIV best
Judges 20:15	*eklektos*	KJV chosen	NKJV select	NIV chosen
Judges 20:34	*eklektos*	KJV chosen	NKJV select	NIV finest
1 Samuel 24:2	*eklektos*	KJV three thousand men chosen		
1 Samuel 26:2	*eklektos*	KJV three thousand men chosen		
Psalm 89:19	*eklektos*	KJV chosen	NKJV one chosen from	NIV young man

2 Samuel 6:1   *neanias* – young man
Also in 1 Kings 12:21

2 Chronicles 11:1   *neaniskos* – young man
Also in Jeremiah 49:19 (LXX29:19), 50:44 (LXX2:44)

Proverbs 22:1 Portion of verse not translated

Excellent

Song of Solomon 5:15   *eklektos*   KJV "excellent as the
                                                        cedars"

Require

2 Samuel 19:38   *eklegó*

BACHAR Conclusion

It can readily be seen that BACHAR means "To choose" by the very
regular use of *eklegó*.

However, it can also be readily seen that *neanias* which means
"young man" is used to translate it and *eklektos* which as we saw
has 52 undisputed references to "quality" elsewhere. So that it is
reasonable to consider that where it is translated as *eklektos* the LXX
translators of the Hebrew saw and wanted to interpret BACHAR as
"quality".

BARAR

BARAR is found in the KJV variously in regards to its root meaning of "to clarify", "to examine" or, "test". Thus anything "chosen" is due to its quality being discovered (after a testing).

This automatically gives us a **new tally:** quality (type) 62; chosen 8; elect 4; choose 1

BARAR Translations

However, let's take a closer look at BARAR where it is translated as follows in the KJV and see the counterpart in the LXX. The following thereby identifies which Greek word was used in the LXX portion for the Hebrew word used. First comes the English word in alphabetical order as found in the KJV, then under each English word comes the Greek word in alphabetical order used to translate the Hebrew word BARAR in the LXX. In bold are the instances where *eklektos* are found.

Appoint

| Ezekiel 21:19 | *diatassó* | |

Make bright

| Jeremiah 51:11 | *paraskeuadzó* | |

Choice

| 1 Chronicles 7:40 | *eklektos* | **KJV choice *and* mighty men** |
| Nehemiah 5:18 | *eklektos* | **KJV six choice sheep** |

Chosen

| 1 Chronicles 16:41 | *eklegó* | |
| 1 Chronicles 9:22 | *eklektos* | **KJV chosen to be porters** |

Be clean

| Isaiah 52:11 | Translated differently as "separate yourselves" *aphoridzó* |

Cleanse
Jeremiah 4:11   *katharos*

Clearly
Job 33:3   *katharos*

Manifest
Ecclesiastes 3:18   *diakrinó*

Polished
Isaiah 49:2   ***eklektos***   **KJV a polished shaft**

Pure
2 Samuel 22:27   ***eklektos***   **KJV with the pure**
2 Samuel 22:27   ***eklektos***   **KJV shew thyself pure**
Psalm 18:26   ***eklektos***   **KJV with the pure**
Psalm 18:26   ***eklektos***   **KJV shew thyself pure**

Zephaniah 3:9   Portion of verse translated differently

Purge
Ezekiel 20:38   *eklegó*

Be purified
Daniel 12:10   *eklegó*

BARAR Conclusion

BARAR can readily be seen to be about purging, cleaning, making pure. Anything chosen is readily understood so because it is made fit by being clean or pure. It is reasonable to see here that *eklektos* is used by the translator to identify quality with "pure", "polished" and "choice sheep".

BACHIR

The remainder of times *eklektos* is found un the LXX it is translated from BACHIR.

What is interesting and significant when looking at the above translations for BACHAR and BARAR is that where quality is meant *eklektos* is readily used, but when a choosing is involved ready use is made of the Greek verbs for that purpose.

This makes this next word BACHIR appear odd and out of place. Because there is no exception and every single place it is found in the Hebrew has been translated in the LXX as *eklektos*.

Could it be the Septuagint translators felt that BACHIR was always about quality?

It looks that way. And this brings into question the meaning of BACHIR and its translation in the Old Testament itself. Since with every place it occurs it is always translated as *eklektos* in the LXX.

Certainly due to the striking variance of this Hebrew word from the ready pattern throughout the LXX demonstrated brings me to the following conclusion: there is an error possibility in the appreciation of BACHIR in the translation of the Hebrew into the modern languages or the LXX translators by the clear pattern elsewhere misread it as for quality. And it is because of this clear and distinct variance that BACHIR is not useable as a true representation from the rest of the LXX witness about *eklektos*.

Chosen

1 Chronicles 16:13	*eklektos*
Psalm 89:3	*eklektos*
Psalm 105:6	*eklektos*
Psalm 105:43	*eklektos*
Psalm 106:5	*eklektos*
Psalm 106:23	*eklektos*
Isaiah 43:20	*eklektos*
Isaiah 65:15	*eklektos*

Choose

2 Samuel 21:6	*eklektos*

Elect

Isaiah 42:1	*eklektos*
Isaiah 45:4	*eklektos*
Isaiah 65:9	*eklektos*
Isaiah 65:22	*eklektos*

ROBERT YOUNG and BACHIR

Robert Young in his concordance makes the following interpretation of BACHIR which also points to quality in view: "choice, chosen, tried one". But, for an internal pointer to the "chosen" or "elect" appreciation as the incorrect one for BACHIR I also offer the following thinking.

As the word "elect" is used from BACHIR here we see it as a reference to Jesus prophetically, as Jesus is God in the flesh we see the "chosen" emphasis in trouble.

> Behold! My Servant whom I uphold, My Elect One *in whom*
> My soul delights! I have put My Spirit upon Him; He will
> bring forth justice to the Gentiles.   *Isaiah 42:1*

Even when we see it as a reference to Israel as a people and nation it is told us repeatedly that only the faithful in the midst will make it and be recognised in the end as a part of God's kingdom. Paul said the same thing. Here are 3 examples of the word BACHIR for the people of Israel which I will follow with a couple to show that only the faithful – the quality guys in the midst – are seen as relevant.

> For Jacob My servant's sake, and Israel My elect, I have even
> called you by your name; I have named you, though you
> have not known Me.   *Isaiah 45:4*

> I will bring forth descendants from Jacob, and from Judah
> an heir of My mountains; My elect shall inherit it, and My
> servants shall dwell there.   *Isaiah 65:9*

> They shall not build and another inhabit; they shall not
> plant and another eat; for as the days of a tree, *so shall be*
> the days of My people, and My elect shall long enjoy the
> work of their hands.   *Isaiah 65:22*

And now for a couple of quotes to show it is only the faithful within the midst of Israel that are seen as relevant.

> "Therefore I will judge you, O house of Israel, every one according to his ways," says the Lord GOD. "Repent, and turn from all your transgressions, so that iniquity will not be your ruin. Cast away from you all the transgressions which you have committed, and get yourselves a new heart and a new spirit. For why should you die, O house of Israel? For I have no pleasure in the death of one who dies," says the Lord GOD. "Therefore turn and live!"   *Ezekiel 18:30-32*

And in Paul's writing,

> For he is not a Jew who *is one* outwardly, nor *is* that circumcision *which is* outward in the flesh; but *he is* a Jew who *is one* inwardly; and circumcision *is that* of the heart, in the Spirit, *and* not in the letter; whose praise *is not* from men but from God.   *Romans 2:28-29*

So a choice of God is not what is seen by "elect" from BACHIR, but the quality person or persons. Not that Israel as a people are not chosen out from other nations, but that it is the righteous, the faithful, in the midst that will benefit as God has chosen them first to show His name through. The rest of us who are faithful will then join them at Jesus' return. For elect from BACHIR to mean chosen rather than quality these truths are at issue. Can it be that like the English has no direct equivalent adjective for a person to mean "quality" so Hebrew has not also, so that as regards people BACHIR was used?

Conclusion

Suffice to say that in the 1st century a reader of the New Testament had knowledge of the Greek as found in the LXX. Seeing as this

245

Old Testament Version had the fat cows that came out of the Nile in Pharaoh's dream which Joseph interpreted as *eklektos* cows. And that quality silver is *eklektos* silver. And young men (guys in their prime) are known as *eklektos*. When he read in Matthew that Jesus said "Many are called, few *eklektos*" he fully understood that few were quality and fit for that calling. In Luke 23:35, 1 Peter 2:4 and 1 Peter 2:6 Jesus is referred to as "chosen" and "elect" from the word *eklektos*, since He is God in the flesh (1 Timothy 3:16), it is not a reference to His being picked from others, but His being Special.

Notes

1   As stated in the Introduction in Greek there are 2 "o"s as letters: *omicron* and *omega*. I denote *omicron* with an ordinary "*o*" and *omega* with "*ó*". Similarly there is *epsilon* and *eta*. I denote *epsilon* with an ordinary "*e*" and *eta* with "*é*".

2   The initial list worked from was taken from A CON-CORDANCE OF THE SEPTUAGINT compiled by George Morrish and published by Zondervan. First published in 1887.

3   Both Greek words and the initial translation quoted are taken from THE SEPTUAGINT WITH APOCRYPHA: GREEK AND ENGLISH by Sir Lancelot C.L. Brenton and published by Hendrikson. Originally published in1851.

4   The following symbols have been used to identify which Hebrew word "chosen", "elect", "choose" and "excellent" were translated from: *bachar; †bachir; ‡bachur; ^barar; °mibchar.

5   YOUNG'S literal translation of the HOLY BIBLE by Robert Young Revised Edition published by Baker Book House. Third Edition January 1898.

GENEA

Septuagint examples of *genea* as other than "generation"
In chapter 3 entitled *Incorrect Word Meanings* I introduced the Septuagint as a valuable source for discovering the meaning of words used in the New Testament. Here follows the examples of *genea* not meaning "generation" in the Septuagint alongside the translated Hebrew words found in English versions: NKJV, KJV, NIV, NLT as appropriate.

Explicit examples of "Related Group" from *genea* in the LXX

Quick List

People of his time NIV	*genea*	Genesis 6:9
(their) **Birth** NIV	*geneón*	Genesis 25:13
(your) **kindred**	*genean*	Genesis 31:3
kindred	*genean*	Genesis 43:7
(their) **people**	*geneas*	Leviticus 20:18
Descendants NIV	*geneai*	Leviticus 23:43
Descendants NIV	*geneas*	Leviticus 25:30
Family – clan NIV	*genean*	Leviticus 25:41
Posterity	*geneais*	Numbers 9:10
kinsmen - kindred KJV	*genean*	Numbers 10:30
Descendants - children KJV	*geneai*	Numbers 13:22
Descendants - children KJV	*genean*	Numbers 13:28
Descendants NIV + NLT	*geneais*	Joshua 22:28
Descendants - seed KJV	*geneón*	Esther 9:28
(the) **Company** NIV	*genea*	Psalm 14:5
(Offspring) LXX only	*genea*	Proverbs 22:4
Descendants NIV + NLT	*genean*	Isaiah 53:8
Family - nation NIV	*geneas*	Jeremiah 8:3
Families - peoples NIV	*geneas*	Jeremiah 10:25

Expanded Version of *genea* Quick List
(with Strong's Numbers: Ss) for the Hebrew word from
which it was translated

Genesis 6:9	*en té* **genea**	perfect in his generations (=KJV) blameless among... the **people of his time** NIV **Ss1755**
Genesis 25:13	*tón* **geneón** *auton*	And these were the names of the sons of Ishmael, by their names, according to their generations listed in the order of their **birth** NIV **Ss8435**
Genesis 31:3	*eis tén* **genean** *sou*	and to your **kindred** (= KJV) - later NKJV **family relatives** NIV **Ss4138**
Genesis 43:7	*tén* **genean** *hémón*	asked us pointedly about ourselves and our **kindred** (=KJV) - later NKJV **family** (=NIV) **Ss4138**
Leviticus 20:18	*ek tés* **geneas** *autón*	shall be cut off from their **people** (=KJV) **Ss5971** – **people** NIV
Leviticus 23:43	*hai* **geneai** *humón*	that your generations may know that I made (=KJV) "that your **posterity** may see that I made the children of Israel to dwell in tents" LXX translation

		so that your **descendants** will know NIV **Ss1755**
Leviticus 25:30	*eis tas* **geneas** *autou*	him who bought it, throughout his generations (=KJV) shall belong permanently to the buyer... and his **descendants**. NIV **Ss1755**
Leviticus 25:41	*eis tén* **genean** *autou*	and shall return to his own **family** (=KJV) To his own **clan** NIV **Ss4940**
Numbers 9:10	*en tais* **geneais** *humón*	If anyone of you or your **posterity** (= KJV) **Descendants** NIV **Ss1755**
Numbers 10:30	*eis tén* **genean** *mou*	I will depart to my *own* land and to my **kinsmen** Later NKJV **relatives** - **kindred** KJV **Ss4138** **people** NIV
Numbers 13:22 (23LXX)	**geneai** *Enach*	the **descendants** of Anak, *were* there (=NIV) **children** KJV **Ss3211**
Numbers 13:28 (29LXX)	*kai tén* **genean**	we saw the **descendants** of Anak there (=NIV) **children** KJV **Ss3211**
Joshua 22:28	*tais* **geneais** *hémón*	when they say *this* to us or to our generations... in time to come (=KJV) "that they should speak

so to us, or to our **posterity** hereafter" LXX translation or to our **descendants** NIV (= NLT) **Ss 1755**

Esther 9:28	*ek tón* **geneón**	should not perish among their **descendants seed** KJV **Ss2233**
Psalm 14:5 (13:5LXX)	*en* **genea** *dikaia*	For God *is* with the generation of the righteous (= KJV) in the **company** of the righteous NIV **Ss1755**
Proverbs 22:4	**Genea** *sophias*	"The fear of the Lord is the **offspring** of wisdom, and wealth, and glory, and life." This is not in the Hebrew (Hence no Ss number) - This is in the Hebrew: By humility *and* the fear of the LORD *are* riches and honor and life.
Isaiah 53:8	*tén* **genean** *autou*	And who will declare His generation? (= KJV) And who can speak of his **descendants**? NIV (=NLT) **Ss1755**
Jeremiah 8:3	*apo tés* **geneas** *ekeinés*	of those who remain of this evil **family** (=KJV) **Ss4940** - **nation** NIV (=NLT)

| Jeremiah 10:25 | *kai epi* **geneas** *hai* | And on the **families** who do not call on Your name (=KJV) **Ss4940 - peoples** NIV (=NLT) |

Full List of *genea* in the LXX

Where 2X *genea* is used – one following another – to mean "*generations*" or "*never*", etc, except where indicated, the word is placed in italics in the NKJV quote and followed by (*X2*). All other italics are as per the NKJV. Bible references in brackets indicate the word *genea* is in the LXX with no counterpart in the Hebrew text being translated: the translation for these is a separate translation of the LXX and not of the Hebrew.

Genesis 6:9	*genea*	perfect in his generations (=KJV) blameless among the **people** of his time NIV
Genesis 7:1	*té genea tauté*	you *are* righteous before Me in this generation
Genesis 9:12	*eis geneas aiónious*	this *is* the sign . . . for perpetual generations
Genesis 15:16	*Tetarté de genea*	But in the fourth generation they shall return
Genesis 17:7	*eis tas geneas autón*	after you in their generations
Genesis 17:9	*tas geneas autón*	throughout their generations
(Genesis 17:10)	*tas geneas autón*	LXX only and adds words after the Hebrew translated words: your descendants after you – thy seed after thee (KJV) with "for their generations"
Genesis 17:12	*eis tas geneas humón*	every male child in your generations

Genesis 25:13	*tón geneón auton*	And these were the names of the sons of Ishmael… by their names, according to their generations listed in the order of their **birth** NIV
Genesis 31:3	*eis tén genean sou*	and to your **kindred/ family – relatives** NIV
Genesis 43:7	*tén genean hémón*	asked us pointedly about ourselves and our **kindred**
Genesis 50:23	*heós trités geneas*	Joseph saw Ephraim's children to the third *generation*
Exodus 1:6	*hé genea ekeiné*	And Joseph died, all his brothers, and all that generation
Exodus 3:15	*kai mnémosunon geneón*	
Ibid.	*geneais*	and this *is* My memorial to all *generations* (*X2*)
Exodus 12:14	*pasas tas geneas humón*	throughout your generations
Exodus 12:17	*eis geneas humón*	observe this day throughout your generations
Exodus 12:42	*eis geneas autón*	for all the children of Israel throughout their generations
(Exodus 13:18)	*pempté de genea anebésan hoi huioi Israél ek gés Aiguptou*	LXX only "and in the fifth generation the children of Israel went up out of the land of Egypt."
Exodus 16:32	*eis tas geneas humón*	to be kept for your generations

Exodus 16:33	*eis tas geneas humón*	to be kept for your generations
Exodus 17:16	*apo geneón*	the LORD *will have* war with Amalek
Ibid.	*eis geneas*	from generation to generation
Exodus 20:5	*kai tetartés geneas*	to the third and fourth *generations*
Exodus 27:21	*eis tas geneas humón*	*It shall be* a statute forever to their generations
Exodus 29:42	*eis geneas humón*	throughout your generations
Exodus 30:8	*eis geneas autón*	before the LORD throughout your generations
Exodus 30:10	*eis geneas autón*	upon it throughout your generations
Exodus 30:21	*autó kai tais geneais autou met' auton*	to him and his descendants throughout… their generations.
Exodus 30:31	*eis tas geneas humón*	a holy anointing oil to Me throughout your generations
Exodus 31:13	*eis tas geneas humón*	a sign between Me and you… throughout your generations
Exodus 31:16	*eis tas geneas autón*	to observe the Sabbath throughout their generations
Exodus 34:7	*kai tetartén genean*	to the third and the fourth generation
Exodus 40:15	*eis tas geneas autón*	an everlasting priesthood… throughout their generations
Leviticus 3:17	*eis tas geneas humón*	a perpetual statute throughout your generations
Leviticus 6:18	*eis tas geneas humón*	a statute forever in your generations

Leviticus 7:36 (26LXX)	*eis tas geneas autón*	a statute forever throughout their generations
Leviticus 10:9	*eis tas geneas humón*	*It shall be* a statute forever… throughout your generations
Leviticus 17:7	*eis tas geneas humón*	a statute forever for them… throughout their generations
Leviticus 20:18	*ek tés geneas autón*	shall be cut off from their **people** (=NIV)
Leviticus 21:17	*eis tas geneas humón*	of your descendants in *succeeding* generations
Leviticus 22:3	*eis tas geneas humón*	of all your descendants throughout your generations
Leviticus 23:14	*eis tas geneas humón*	a statute forever throughout your generations
Leviticus 23:21	*eis tas geneas humón*	in all your dwellings throughout your generations
Leviticus 23:31	*eis tas geneas humón*	a statute forever throughout your generations
Leviticus 23:41	*eis tas geneas humón*	a statute forever in your generations
Leviticus 23:43	*hai geneai humón*	that your generations may know that I made "that your **posterity** may see that I made the children of Israel to dwell in tents" LXX translation so your **descendants** will know NIV
Leviticus 24:3	*eis tas geneas humón*	a statute forever in your generations

Leviticus 25:30	*eis tas geneas autou*	to him who bought it, throughout his generations shall belong permanently to the buyer and his **descendants**. NIV
Leviticus 25:41	*eis tén genean autou*	and shall return to his own **family** (=KJV) To his own **clan** NIV
Numbers 9:10	*en tais geneais humón*	If anyone of you or your **posterity** **Descendants** NIV
Numbers 10:8	*eis tas geneas humón*	as an ordinance forever throughout your generations
Numbers 10:30	*eis tén genean mou*	I will depart to my *own* land and to my **kinsmen** I am going back to my own land… and my own **people** NIV
Numbers 13:22 (23LXX)	*geneai Enach*	the **descendants** of Anak, *were* there (=NIV)
Numbers 13:28 (29LXX)	*kai tén genean Enach*	we saw the **descendants** of Anak there
Numbers 14:18	*kai tetartés geneas*	to the third and fourth *generation*
Numbers 15:14	*en tais geneais humón*	whoever *is* among you throughout your generations
Numbers 15:15	*eis tas geneas humón*	an ordinance forever throughout your generations
Numbers 15:21	*eis tas geneas humón*	a heave offering throughout your generations

Numbers 15:23	*eis tas geneas humón*	and onward throughout your generations
Numbers 15:38	*eis tas geneas autón*	of their garments throughout their generations
Numbers 18:23	*eis tas geneas autón*	a statute forever, throughout your generations
Numbers 32:13	*pasa hé genea*	forty years, until all the generation that had done
Numbers 35:29	*eis tas geneas humón*	judgment to you throughout your generations
Deuteronomy 2:14	*pasa genea andrón*	until all the generation of the men of war
Deuteronomy 5:9	*kai tetartén genean*	to the third and fourth *generations*
Deuteronomy 7:9	*eis chilias geneas*	covenant and mercy for a thousand generations
Deuteronomy 23:3	*heós dekatés geneas*	even to the tenth generation none
Deuteronomy 23:8	*autois, geneas trité*	The children of the third generation
Deuteronomy 29:22	*hé genea hé etera*	so that the coming generation of your children
Deuteronomy 32:5	*genea skolia*	A perverse and crooked generation
Deuteronomy 32:7	*eté geneón*	Remember the days of old,
Ibid.	*geneais*	Consider the years *of many generations* (X2)
Deuteronomy 32:20	*hoti genea exestrammené*	For they *are* a perverse generation
(Joshua 22:27)	*tén geneón hémón*	witness between you and us and… our generations after us "between our **posterity** after us" LXX translation

Joshua 22:28	*tais geneais hémón*	when they say *this* to us or to our generations… in time to come "that they should speak *so* to us, or to our **posterity** hereafter" LXX translation If they ever say this to us, or to our **descendants** NIV
Judges 2:10	*kai pasa hé genea ekeiné*	When all that generation had been gathered… to their fathers
Ibid. 2:10	*kai anesté genea hetera*	another generation arose after them… who did not know the LORD
Judges 3:2	*plén dia tas geneas*	so that the generations of the children of Israel… might be taught to know war
1 Chronicles 16:15	*eis chilias geneas*	which He commanded, for a thousand generations
Esther 9:28 (27LXX)	*kata genean*	these days *should be* remembered and kept
Ibid.	*kai genean*	*throughout every generation (X2)*
Ibid. (28LXX)	*ek tón geneón*	should not perish among their **descendants**
Job 8:8	*gar genean prótén*	For inquire, please, of the former age
Job 42:16	*tetartén genean*	and grandchildren *for* four generations
Psalm 10:6 (9:6LXX)	*apo geneas*	He has said in his heart, "I shall not be moved;
Ibid.	*eis geneas*	I shall *never* be in adversity."

Psalm 12:7 (11:7LXX)	*apo tés geneas tautés*	You shall preserve them from this generation forever
Psalm 14:5 (13:5LXX)	*en genea dikaia*	For God *is* with the generation of the righteous – in the **company** of the righteous NIV
Psalm 22:30 (21:30LXX)	*tó Kurió genea hé*	It will be recounted of the Lord to the *next* generation
Psalm 24:6 (23:6LXX)	*hauté hé genea*	This *is* Jacob, the generation of those who seek Him
Psalm 33:11 (32:11LXX)	*apo geneón*	The plans of His heart…
Ibid.	*eis geneas*	*to all generations (X2)*
Psalm 45:17 (44:17LXX)	*en pasé genea*	I will make Your name to be remembered…
Ibid.	*kai genea*	*in all generations (X2)*
Psalm 48:13 (47:13LXX)	eis geneas heteran	That you may tell *it* to the generation following
Psalm 49:11 (48:11LXX)	*eis genean*	Their dwelling places…
Ibid.	*kai genean*	*to all generations (X2)*
Psalm 49:19 (48:19LXX)	*heós geneas paterón*	He shall go to the generation of his fathers
Psalm 61:6 (60:6LXX)	*heós hémeras geneas*	You will prolong the king's life…
Ibid.	*kai geneas*	His years *as many generations (X2)*
Psalm 71:18 (70:18LXX)	*pasé té genea*	Until I declare Your strength to *this* generation
Psalm 72:5 (71:5LXX)	*geneas*	As long as the sun and moon endure…
Ibid.	*geneón*	*Throughout all generations (X2)*
Psalm 73:15 (72:15LXX)	*té genea tón huión*	to the generation of Your children

Psalm 77:8 (76:8LXX)	*apo geneas*	Has His mercy ceased forever?. . .
Ibid.	*kai geneas*	Has *His* promise failed *forevermore*? (X2)
Psalm 78:4 (77:4LXX)	*eis genean heteran*	Telling to the generation to come the praises of
Psalm 78:6 (77:6LXX)	*an gnó genea hetera*	That the generation to come might know *them*
Psalm 78:8 (77:8LXX)	*genea skolia*	A stubborn and rebellious generation
Ibid.	*genea hétis ou*	A generation that did not set its heart aright
Psalm 79:13 (78:13LXX)	*eis genean*	We will show forth Your praise…
Ibid.	*kai genean*	*to all generations* (X2)
Psalm 85:5 (84:5LXX)	*apo geneas*	Will You prolong Your anger…
Ibid.	eis *genean*	*to all generations?* (X2)
Psalm 89:1 (88:1LXX)	eis *genean*	I make known Your faithfulness…
Ibid.	*kai genean*	*to all generations* (X2)
Psalm 89:4 (88:4LXX)	*eis genean*	Your seed I will establish forever…
Ibid.	*kai genean*	And build up your throne *to all generations* (X2)
Psalm 90:1 (89:1LXX)	*en genea*	Lord, You have been our dwelling place…
Ibid.	*kai genea*	*in all generations* (X2)
Psalm 95:10 (94:10LXX)	*té genea ekeiné*	For forty years I was grieved with *that* generation
Psalm 100:5 (99:5LXX)	*kai heós geneas*	And His truth *endures*…
Ibid.	*kai geneas*	*to all generations* (X2)
Psalm 102:12 (101:12LXX)	*eis genean*	And the remembrance of Your name…
Ibid.	*kai genean*	*to all generations* (X2)
Psalm 102:18 (101:18LXX)	*eis genean heteran*	This will be written for the generation to come

Psalm 102:24 (101:24LXX)	*en genea*	Your years *are* throughout…
Ibid.	*geneón*	*all generations (X2)*
Psalm 105:8 (104:8LXX)	*eis chilias geneas*	The word *which* He commanded… for a thousand generations
Psalm 106:31 (105:31LXX)	*eis genean*	And that was accounted to him for righteousness…
Ibid.	*kai genean*	*To all generations* forevermore *(X2)*
Psalm 109:13 (108:13LXX)	*en genea mia*	*And* in the generation… following let their name be blotted out
Psalm 112:2 (111:2LXX)	*genea eutheón*	The generation of the upright will be blessed
Psalm 119:90 (118:90LXX)	*eis genean*	Your faithfulness *endures…*
Ibid.	*kai genean*	*to all generations (X2)*
Psalm 135:13 (134:13LXX)	*eis genean*	Your fame, O LORD…
Ibid.	*kai genean*	*throughout all generations (X2)*
Psalm 145:4 (144:4LXX)	*Genea*	One *generation* shall praise…
Ibid.	*kai genea*	Your works *to another (X2)*
Psalm 145:13 (144:13LXX)	*en pasé genea*	And Your dominion *endures…*
Ibid.	*kai genea*	*throughout all generations (X2)*
Psalm 146:10 (145:10LXX)	*eis genean*	Your God, O Zion…
Ibid.	*kai genean*	*to all generations (X2)*
Proverbs 22:4 (LXX only)	*Genea sophias*	"The fear of the Lord is the **offspring** of wisdom, and wealth, and glory, and life." LXX translation

		This is not in the Hebrew – This is: By humility *and* the fear of the LORD *are* riches and honor and life.
Proverbs 27:24	*ek geneas*	Nor does a crown *endure…*
Ibid.	*eis genean*	*to all generations* (*X2*)
Ecclesiastes 1:4	*Genea poreuetai*	*One* generation passes away…
Ibid.	*kai genea erchetai*	and *another* generation comes
Isaiah 13:20	*dia pollón geneón*	Nor will it be settled from generation to generation
Isaiah 24:22	*dia pollón geneón*	After many days they will be punished. "After many generations they shall be visited" LXX translation
Isaiah 34:10	*eis geneas autés*	From generation to generation it shall lie waste
Isaiah 34:17	*geneas*	They shall possess it forever; from generation…
Ibid.	*geneón*	to generation they shall dwell in it
Isaiah 41:4	*autén apo geneón*	Calling the generations from the beginning
Isaiah 51:8	*eis geneas*	And My salvation from generation…
Ibid.	*geneón*	to generation
Isaiah 51:9	*hós genea aiónos*	In the generations of old
Isaiah 53:8	*tén genean autou*	And who will declare His generation? And who can speak of his **descendants**? NIV

Isaiah 58:12	sou aiónia *geneón*	You shall raise up…
Ibid.	*geneais*	the foundations *of many generations* (*X2*)
Isaiah 60:15	euphrosunén *geneón*	A joy *of many*…
Ibid.	*geneais*	*generations* (*X2*)
Isaiah 61:3	*geneai dikaiosunés*	That they may be called trees of righteousness "and they shall be called generations of righteousness" LXX translation
Isaiah 61:4	*eis geneas*	The desolations of many generations
Jeremiah 7:29	*tén genean*	and forsaken the generation of His wrath
Jeremiah 8:3	*apo tés geneas ekeinés*	of those who remain of this evil **family** – this evil **nation** NIV
Jeremiah 10:25	*kai epi geneas hai*	And on the **families** who do not call on Your name The **peoples** who do not call on your name NIV
Lamentations 5:19	*eis genean*	Your throne from generation…
Ibid.	*kai genean*	to generation
Daniel 4:3 (3:33LXX)	*eis genean*	And His dominion *is* from generation…
Ibid.	*kai genean*	to generation
Daniel 4:34 (4:31LXX)	*eis genean*	And His kingdom *is* from generation…
Ibid.	*kai genean*	to generation
Joel 1:3	*eis genean heteran*	And their children another generation
Joel 2:2	*eis geneas*	Even for many successive…
Ibid.	*geneón*	*generations* (*X2*)
Joel 3:20	*eis geneas*	And Jerusalem from generation…

Ibid.	*geneón*	to generation
Zephaniah 3:9	*eis geneas autés*	For then I will restore to the peoples a pure language "For then I will turn to the peoples a tongue for her generation" LXX translation

An example of *genea* translated from
2 different words in the same verse – Esther 9:28

NKJV

that these days *should be* remembered and kept throughout every **generation**, every family, every province, and every city, that these days of Purim should not fail *to be observed* among the Jews, and *that* the memory of them should not perish among their **descendants**.

KJV

And *that* these days *should be* remembered and kept throughout every **generation(Ss1755)**, every family(Ss 4940), every province, and every city; and *that* these days of Purim should not fail from among the Jews, nor the memorial of them perish from their **seed(Ss2233)**.

LXX

*Hai de hémerai autoi mnémosunon epiteloumenon kata **genean** kai* **genean**, *kai polin, kai patrian, kai chóran. Hai de hémerai autai tón phrourai achthésontai eis ton hapanta chronon, kai to mnémosunon autón ou mé eklipé ek tón **geneón***

As you see the two different Strong numbers are for the separate Hebrew words from which "generation" and "seed" have been translated in the KJV. In the Septuagint both different Hebrew words have been translated by the same Greek word and this is the sole passage where *genea* can be seen with both meanings. A clear indicator that two separate meanings was understood by the same translator for the one Greek word.

Simple reason for reconsidering *genea* in the New Testament

The truth of *genea* being used for 2 different concepts can simply be seen in Esther 9:28 where 2 wholly different Hebrew words are seen translated by the same Greek word. This is no different to the English word "table" where one context would see us understand this well as the item of furniture with legs that stands a distance from the floor on which it sits, whilst another context sees it as a reference to a guide: a set of rules or schematics. So that the following sentence would include both and though the word looks the same 2 different meanings are understood:

"The table of contents for the book were typed up on a sheet of paper lying on the kitchen table."

It is up to the context therefore to reveal the meaning meant by the author and with the bible considered as authored not just by the human author of the section in which the word is found, where the context is ambiguous, then other passages touching on the same subject matter help reveal which of the two meanings is meant.

TASSÓ

The Septuagint

Here are all the examples of *tassó* in the Septuagint. I count 60 examples of the verb *tassó* translated from various Hebrew words for which I also provide the **S**trong numbers (**Ss**) where applicable. The initial translation is of the LXX. Where added the next translation/s are of the Hebrew.

LXX:

Genesis 3:24 (V.25 in LXX)	*etaxe*	and **stationed** the cherubs "and he **placed** at the east of the garden of Eden Cherubims" KJV, "**placed**" NKJV (**Ss7931**)
Exodus 8:9	*taxai*	**appoint** me *a time* when I shall pray "when shall I entreat for thee" KJV, "Accept the honor of saying when I shall intercede for you" NKJV
Exodus 8:12	*etaxato*	as Pharao **appointed** him (not in Heb - nih)
Exodus 29:43	*taxomai*	And I will there **give orders** to the children of Israel (nih)
1 Samuel 20:35	*etaxato*	and Jonathan went out to the field, as he

		appointed *to do* for a signal[1] to David ([1]a witness- lit) – "at the time **appointed with David**" KJV, NKJV (Ss4150)
1 Samuel 22:7	*taxei*	will he **make** you all captains of hundreds and captains of thousands "**make**" KJV, NKJV (Ss7760 - to set)
2 Samuel 7:11	*etaxa*	from the days when I **appointed** judges over my people Israel "**commanded**" KJV, NKJV (Ss6680)
2 Samuel 20:5	*etaxato*	delayed beyond the time which David **appointed** him "**appointed**" KJV, NKJV (Ss3259)
2 Samuel 23:23	*etaxen*	David **made** him his reporter "**appointed**" NKJV, "**set** him" KJV (Ss7760)
1 Kings 2:5	*etaxe*	and **shed** the blood of war in peace [Gk. ordered] "**shed**" KJV, NKJV [Heb. KJV margin "**put**"] (Ss7760)
2 Kings 10:24	*etaxen*	And Ju **set** for himself eighty men without "**appointed**" NKJV, KJV (Ss7760)
2 Kings 10:27	*etaxan*	and **made** his house a draught house

"**made**" KJV, NKJV (**Ss7760**)

2 Kings 12:17	*etaxen*	and Azael **set** his face to go against Jerusalem "**set**" KJV, NKJV (**Ss7760**)
1 Chronicles16:4	*etaxe*	And he **appointed** before the ark of the covenant of the Lord, Levites to minister – "**appointed**" NKJV, KJV (**Ss5414**)
1 Chronicles 16:7	*etaxe*	Then David first **gave orders** to praise the Lord by the hand of Asaph "**delivered**" KJV, NKJV (**Ss5414**)
1 Chronicles 17:10	*etaxa*	and from the days when I **appointed** judges over my people Israel "**commanded**" KJV, NKJV (**Ss6680**)
2 Chronicles 31:2	*etaxen*	And Ezekias **appointed** the courses of the priests and the Levites "**appointed**" NKJV, KJV (**Ss5975**)
Esther 1:6	*tetamenois*	which was **adorned** with hangings of fine linen and flax on cords of fine linen and purple – "**fastened**" KJV, NKJV (**Ss270**) [the translator for the

		LXX perhaps pictured these as "**arranged**" hence used *tassó*]
Job 14:13	*taxé*	and thou shouldest **set** me a time in which "**appoint**" KJV, NKJV (**Ss7896**)
Job 30:22	*etaxas*	and thou hast **put** me to grief – not equivalent to Hebrew.
Job 31:24	*etaxa*	If I **made** gold my treasure "If I have **made** gold my hope" KJV, NKJV (**Ss7760**)
Job 36:13	*taxousi*	And the hypocrites in heart will **array** wrath *against themselves* "**heap up** wrath" KJV, "**store up** wrath" NKJV (**Ss7760**)
Song of Solomon 2:4	*taxate*	**set** love before me – not equivalent to Hebrew
Song of Solomon 6:4 (6:3LXX)	*tetagmenai*	terrible as *armies* **set** in array "awesome as *an army* with banners" [again an arranged/lined up army is in view]
Song of Solomon 6:10 (6:9LXX)	*tetagmenai*	terrible as *armies* **set** in array "awesome as *an army* with banners" [ditto]

Reference	Greek	Text
Isaiah 38:1	*taxai*	Thus saith the Lord, **Give orders** concerning thy house "**set** your house in order" NKJV, "**set**" KJV (**Ss6680**)
Jeremiah 2:15	*etaxan*	which have **made** his land a wilderness "**made** his land waste" KJV, NKJV (**Ss7896**)
Jeremiah 3:19	*taxó*	**I will set** thee among children "**put**" KJV, NKJV (**Ss7896**)
Jeremiah 5:22	*taxanta*	who have **set** the sand for a bound to the sea "**placed**" KJV, NKJV (**Ss7760**)
Jeremiah 7:30	*etaxan*	they have **set** their abominations in the house "**set**" KJV, NKJV (**Ss7760**)
Jeremiah 10:22	*taxai*	to **make** the cities of Juda a desolation "**make**" KJV, NKJV (**Ss7760**)
Jeremiah 11:13	*etaxate*	according to the number of the streets of Jerusalem have **ye set up** altars to burn incense to Baal – "**set up**" KJV, NKJV (**Ss7760**)
Jeremiah 18:16	*taxai*	to **make** their land a desolation "**make**" KJV, NKJV (**Ss7760**)

Lamentations 3:21	*taxó*	This will I **lay up** in my heart "**recall**" KJV, NKJV (**Ss7725**) [in the sense of arrange in one's heart]
Ezekiel 4:2	*taxeis*	and **set up** engines round about [engines of war for capturing a walled city] "**place**" NKJV (battering rams against it all around); "**set**" KJV (**Ss7760**)
Ezekiel 14:4	*taxé*	and shall **set** the punishment of his iniquity before his face "**putteth**" KJV; "**puts**" NKJV (**Ss7760**)
Ezekiel 14:7	*taxé*	and **set** before his face the punishment of his iniquity "**putteth**" KJV; "**puts**" NKJV (**Ss7760**)
Ezekiel 16:14	*etaxa*	the comeliness which I **put** upon thee, saith the Lord "**put**" KJV; "**bestowed**" NKJV (**Ss7760**)
Ezekiel 17:5	*etaxen*	he **set** it in a conspicuous place "**set** it like a willow tree" NKJV, "**set**" KJV (**Ss7760**)
Ezekiel 19:5	*etaxen*	she **made** him a lion

"**made**" KJV, NKJV
(**Ss7760**)

Ezekiel 20:28	*etaxan*	and **offered** there a sweet-smelling favour "**made**" KJV, "**sent up**" NKJV (**SS7760**)
Ezekiel 24:7	*tetaxa*	I have **set** it upon a smooth rock "**set**" KJV, NKJV (**Ss7760**)
Ezekiel 40:4	*taxon*	and **lay up** in thine heart all things that I show thee "**set** thine heart upon all that I show thee" KJV; "**fix** your mind on everything I show you" [note: Lit. **set** your heart] – **Ss7760**)
Ezekiel 44:5	*taxon*	**attend** with thine heart "**mark** well" KJV [note: Heb. **Set** thine heart] & NKJV [note: Lit. **set** your heart] (**Ss7760**)
Ezekiel 44:5	*taxeis*	and thou shall **attend** well [Gk. your heart] "**mark** well" KJV [note: Heb. **Set** thine heart] & NKJV (**Ss7760**)
Daniel 6:12	*etaxas*	hast thou not **made** a decree "**signed** a decree" KJV, NKJV (**Ss7560**)
Daniel 11:17	*taxei*	And he shall **set** his face to come in with

		the force of his whole kingdom "**set** his face" KJV, NKJV (**Ss7760**)
Hosea 2:3	*taxó*	and **make** her as a dry land "**set** her like a dry land" KJV, NKJV (**Ss7896**)
Hosea 2:14	*taxó*	and will **make** her as desolate "**bring** her into the wilderness" KJV, NKJV (**Ss3212**)
Micah 5:1	*etaxen*	he has **laid** siege against us - = KJV, NKJV (**Ss7760**)
Habakkuk 1:12	*tetaxas*	thou has **established** it for judgment "**ordained** them for judgment" KJV; "**appointed** them for judgment" NKJV (**Ss7760**)
Habakkuk 2:9	*taxai*	that he may **set** his nest on high = KJV, NKJV (**Ss7760**)
Habakkuk 3:19	*taxei*	and he will perfectly **strengthen** my feet "and he will **make** my feet like hind's *feet*" KJV, "**make** my feet like deer's *feet*" NKJV (**Ss7760**)
Zephaniah 1:14	*tetaktai*	the sound of the day of the Lord is **made** bitter and harsh No equivalent in the Hebrew – it is used

		for the verb for "made" in the English translation of the LXX
Haggai 1:5	*taxate*	**Consider** your ways, I pray you "**consider** your ways" KJV, NKJV [Note in KJV margin: Heb. **Set** your heart on your ways] (**Ss7760**) Young "**set** your heart to your ways"
Zechariah 7:12	*etaxan*	and they **made** their heart disobedient "they **made** their hearts like flint" NKJV, "they **made** their hearts *as* an adamant stone" KJV (**Ss7760**)
Zechariah 7:14	*etaxan*	yea they have **made** the choice land a desolation "they **laid** the pleasant land desolate" KJV, "**made**" NKJV (**Ss7760**)
Zechariah 10:3	*taxei*	and shall **make** them as his goodly horse in war "**made**" KJV, "**make**" NKJV (**Ss7760**)
Zechariah 10:4	*etaxe*	and from him he **set** *the battle in order* – no equivalent section in the Heb.
Malachi 1:3	*etaxa*	and **laid** waste his borders (note in LXX

translation: Lit.
appointed them for
desolation) – "**laid**
waste his mountains
and his heritage"
NKJV, "**laid**" KJV
(**Ss7760**)

33 times *tassó* is translated from the Hebrew word with Strong number 7760 and is explained there as follows:

1) to put, place, set, appoint, make
   a) (Qal)

1) to put, set, lay, put or lay upon, lay (violent) hands on

2) to set, direct, direct toward
   a) to extend (compassion) (fig)

3) to set, ordain, establish, found, appoint, constitute, make, determine, fix

4) to set, station, put, set in place, plant, fix

5) to make, make for, transform into, constitute, fashion, work, bring to pass, appoint, give
   b) (Hiphil) to set or make for a sign
   c) (Hophal) to be set

If the word ARRANGE is in mind as per Young, the verbs in the above OT passages can be pictured accordingly.

Other Greek words unrelated to *tassó* used in the N.T. for "appoint" and "ordain" (KJV)

These verbs are less about the general sense of "to arrange" as Young describes for *tassó*: some are actions of a more direct specific decision; others more loose still. The initial descriptions for the verbs are from Young.

Anadeiknumi – to shew, to point out
Luke 10:1
"after these things the Lord appointed other seventy also" KJV

apokeimai – To be laid off or aside
Hebrews 9:27
"And as it is appointed unto men once to die" KJV

Ginomai – To become
Acts 1:22
"must one be ordained to be a witness" KJV

diatithémi - To put throughout
Luke 22:29
"And I appoint unto you a kingdom as my Father hath appointed unto me" KJV

histémi – To put, place
Acts 1:23
"And they appointed two, Joseph called…" KJV

Also Acts 17:31
"Because he hath appointed a day…" KJV

Horidzó – To mark out or off
Acts 10:42
"it is he which was ordained of God *to be* the Judge of quick and dead" KJV

Also Acts 17:31
"…he will judge the world in righteousness by *that* man whom he hath ordained…" KJV

Kataskeuadzó – To prepare fully
Hebrews 9:6
"Now when these things were thus ordained" KJV

Kathistémi – To place or set down
Acts 6:3
"whom we may appoint over this business" KJV

Titus 1:5
"ordain elders in every city"

Also Hebrews 5:1 and 8:3

Krinó – To judge, decide
Acts 16:4
"that were ordained of the apostles and elders"

poieó – To do, make
Hebrews 3:2
"Who was faithful to him that appointed him" KJV
Also Mark 3:14

prographó – To write or describe before
Jude 4
"who were before ordained of old to this" KJV

proetoimadzó – To make ready before
Ephesians 2:10
"Which God hath before ordained that we" KJV

prooridzó – To mark out publicly or before
1 Corinthians 2:7
"which God ordained before the world unto our glory" KJV

tithémi – To put, place
Matthew 24:51
"and appoint *him* his portion with the" KJV
Also Luke 12:46, John 15:16, 1 Thessalonians 5:9, 1 Timothy 2:7, 2 Timothy 1:11, Hebrews 1:2 and 1 Peter 2:8

Cheirotoneó – To elect by stretching out the hand
Acts 14:23
"And when they had ordained them elders in every church" KJV

ANÉR

The aim of this appendix is to show two things. The same word in Greek is used for either a "husband" or, a "man". And secondly whenever it is a "man", it is always a particular man. So that in plural, it is a particular group of men. It is of note that there is no other Greek word from which to translate the word "husband". This is valuable to correctly understand important passages on the issue of women in leadership.

Here follows the word *anér*. There is another Greek word for man commonly used: *anthrópos*. See the separate appendix for *anthrópos*. The reference is first given in the order as found in the New Testament. Then, the word *anér* in the declension used in the Greek passage. Then the translation in English as found in the NKJV. A few have not been translated in the NKJV and with these I have added in brackets the text in the KJV which shows this appropriately.

It will be readily seen that "husband" or a (particular) man is always the meaning.

N.B. As mentioned in the preface: notes to the book, I use the letter "e" with the acute accent "é" to denote the Greek letter "eta" (the long "e") to differentiate from "epsilon". Similarly I use the letter "o" with the acute accent "ó" to denote the Greek letter "omega" (the long "o") to differentiate from "omicron".

The declensions of *anér* preceded by those of
the definite article (male only)

A declension is the name for the different beginnings and mostly endings of a word to show its relationship with other words in a sentence. The example in English that remains is the genitive case – the name for the relationship of belonging to or, being offspring of. Example: a man's son: where " 's" is the declension of man.

The declensions of the definite article "the" help to identify that the declension for *anér* in the plural nominative is the same as for the plural in the vocative case as found in the New Testament. You may also notice that in highlighting in bold the English translation I also highlight the indefinite article "a". There is no separate word in Greek for "a" and whenever the definite article is not present this is taken by translators from *anér* itself.

The	*ho*	Nominative		singular	*anér*	**man/husband**
	hoi	(the subject)		plural	*andres*	
	ton	Accusative		singular	*andra*	
	tous	(the direct object)		plural	*andras*	
	tó	Dative		singular	*andri*	
	tois	(the indirect object)		plural	*andrasin*	
		for a man/husband				
		– to a man/husband				
	tou	Genitive		singular	*andros*	
	tón	(the belonging to)		plural	*andrón*	
		of a man/husband –				
		a man's/husband's				
	n/a	Vocative		singular	n/a	
	n/a	(the spoken)		plural	*andres*	

Passages of the New Testament with *anér*
The Received Text is used throughout

Matthew	1:16	*ton*	*andra*	Joseph **the husband** of Mary
	1:19	*ho*	*anér*	Then Joseph her **husband**
	7:24		*andri*	**a** wise **man** who built
	7:26		*andri*	**a** foolish **man** who built
	12:41		*Andres*	**The men** of Nineveh will rise
	14:21		*andres*	about five thousand **men**, besides women and children
	14:35	*hoi*	*andres*	when **the men** of that place
	15:38		*andres*	four thousand **men**, besides women and children
Mark	6:20		*andra*	**a** just and holy **man**

	6:44	*andres*	about five thousand **men**
	10:2	*andri*	Is it lawful **for a man** to divorce
	10:12 *ton*	*andra*	if a woman divorces her **husband**
Luke	1:27	*andri*	a virgin betrothed **to a man** whose name
	1:34	*andra*	since I do not know **a man**
	2:36	*andros*	had lived with **a husband** seven years
	5:8	*anér*	for I am **a** sinful **man**
	5:12	*anér*	behold, **a man** who was full of leprosy
	5:18	*andres*	behold, **men** brought on a bed . . .
	7:20 *hoi*	*andres*	When **the men** had come to Him
	8:27	*anér*	there met Him a certain **man** from the city
	8:38 *ho*	*anér*	Now **the man** from whom the demons
	8:41	*anér*	there came **a man** named Jairus
	9:14	*andres*	there were about five thousand **men**
	9:30	*andres*	behold, two **men** talked with Him
	9:32 *tous*	*andras*	and **the** two **men** who stood
	9:38	*anér*	Suddenly **a man** from the multitude
	11:31 *tón*	*andrón*	with **the men** of this generation
	11:32	*andres*	**the men** of Nineveh will rise up
	14:24 *tón*	*andrón*	none **of** those **men** who were invited
	16:18	*andros*	who is divorced from *her* **husband**
	17:12	*andres*	there met Him ten **men** who were lepers
	19:2	*anér*	*there was* **a man** named Zacchaeus
	19:7	*andri*	a guest with **a man** who is a sinner
	22:63 *hoi*	*andres*	Now **the men** who held Jesus mocked
	23:50	*anér*	*there was* **a man** named Joseph, a council member,
	23:50	*anér*	**a** good and just **man**

	24:4		*andres*	behold, two **men** stood by them
John	1:13		*andros*	nor of the will **of man**, but of God
	1:30		*anér*	After me comes **a Man** who is preferred before me
	4:16	*ton*	*andra*	Go, call your **husband**, and come here
	4:17		*andra*	I have no **husband**
	4:17		*andra*	You have well said, 'I have no **husband**'
	4:18		*andras*	you have had five **husbands**
	4:18		*anér*	the one whom you now have is not your **husband**
	6:10	*hoi*	*andres*	**the men** sat down, in number about five thousand
Acts	1:10		*andres*	behold, two **men** stood by them
	1:11		*andres*	**Men** of Galilee, why do you stand
	1:16		*andres*	**Men** *and* brethren, this Scripture
	1:21	*tón*	*andrón*	Therefore, **of** these **men** who have accompanied us
	2:5		*andres*	Jews, devout **men**, from every nation
	2:14		*andres*	**Men** of Judea and all who dwell in Jerusalem
	2:22		*andres*	**Men** of Israel, hear these words
	2:22		*andra*	Jesus of Nazareth, **a Man** attested by God
	2:29		*andres*	**Men** *and* brethren, let *me* speak freely
	2:37		*andres*	**Men** *and* brethren, what shall we do?
	3:2		*anér*	a certain **man** lame from his mother's womb
	3:12		*andres*	**Men** of Israel, why do you marvel
	4:4	*tón*	*andrón*	the number **of the men** came to be about five thousand
	5:1		*anér*	a certain **man** named Ananias
	5:9	*ton*	*andra*	those who have buried your **husband** *are* at the door
	5:10	*ton*	*andra*	buried *her* by her **husband**

5:14		*andrón*	multitudes of both **men** and women
5:25	*hoi*	*andres*	Look, **the men** you put in prison
5:35		*andres*	**Men** of Israel, take heed
5:36		*andrón*	A number **of men**, about four hundred
6:3		*andras*	from among you seven **men** of *good* reputation
6:5		*andra*	Stephen, **a man** full of faith and the Holy Spirit
6:11		*andras*	they secretly induced **men** to say
7:2		*andres*	**Men** and brethren and fathers, listen
7:26		*andres*	**Men**, you are brethren; why do you
8:2		*andres*	And devout **men** carried Stephen *to his burial*
8:3		*andras*	and dragging off **men** and women
8:9		*anér*	there was **a certain man** called Simon
8:12		*andres*	both **men** and women were baptized
8:27		*anér*	behold, **a man** of Ethiopia, a eunuch
9:2		*andras*	whether **men** or women
9:7	*hoi*	*andres*	And **the men** who journeyed with him
9:12		*andra*	in a vision he has seen **a man** named Ananias
9:13	*tou*	*andros*	I have heard from many about this **man**
9:38		*andras*	there, they sent two **men** to him
10:1		*anér*	There was **a certain man** in Caesarea
10:5		*andras*	Now send **men** to Joppa
10:17	*hoi*	*andres*	behold, **the men** who had been sent
10:19		*andres*	Behold, three **men** are seeking you

10:21	*tous*	*andras*	Peter went down to **the men** who had been sent
10:22		*anér*	*the* centurion, **a** just **man**, one who fears God
10:28		*andri*	unlawful it is **for a** Jewish **man** to keep company
10:30		*anér*	behold, **a man** stood before me
11:3		*andras*	You went in to uncircumcised **men** and ate
11:11		*andres*	three **men** stood before the house
11:13		*andras*	Send **men** to Joppa, and call for Simon
11:20		*andres*	some of them were **men** from Cyprus
11:24		*anér*	he was **a** good **man**, full of the Holy Spirit
13:7		*andri*	Sergius Paulus, **an** intelligent **man**
13:15		*andres*	**Men** *and* brethren, if you have
13:16		*andres*	**Men** of Israel, and you who fear God
13:21		*andra*	the son of Kish, **a man** of the tribe
13:22		*andra*	the *son* of Jesse, *a man after My own heart*
13:26		*andres*	**Men** *and* brethren, sons of the family of Abraham
13:38		*andres*	let it be known to you, brethren, that through
			[be it known unto you, **men** *and* brethren, that through KJV]
14:8		*anér*	in Lystra **a** certain **man** without strength
14:15		*andres*	**Men**, why are you doing these things?
15:7		*andres*	**Men** and brethren, you know that a good while
15:13		*andres*	**Men** *and* brethren, listen to me
15:22		*andras*	to send chosen **men** of their own company

15:22		*andras*	and Silas, leading **men** among the brethren
15:25		*andras*	to send chosen **men** to you
16:9		*anér*	**A man** of Macedonia stood and pleaded
17:5		*andras*	some of the evil **men** from the marketplace
17:12		*andrón*	prominent women as well as **men**
17:22		*andres*	**Men** of Athens, I perceive
17:31		*andri*	righteousness by **the Man** whom He has ordained
17:34		*andres*	However, some **men** joined him and believed
18:24		*anér*	an eloquent **man** *and* mighty in the Scriptures
19:7	*hoi*	*andres*	Now **the men** were about twelve in all.
19:25		*andres*	**Men**, you know that we have our prosperity
19:35		*andres*	he said: "**Men** of Ephesus, what
19:37	*tous*	*andras*	you have brought these **men** here who
20:30		*andres*	from among yourselves **men** will rise up
21:11	*ton*	*andra*	bind **the man** who owns this belt
21:23		*andres*	We have four **men** who have taken a vow
21:26	*tous*	*andras*	Then Paul took **the men**, and the next
21:28		*andres*	**Men** of Israel, help! This is
21:38		*andras*	the four thousand assassins [four thousand **men** that were murderers KJV]
22:1		*andres*	**Men**, brethren, and fathers, hear my
22:3		*anér*	I am indeed a Jew, born in Tarsus [I am verily **a man** *which am* a Jew KJV]

22:4		*andras*	delivering into prisons both **men** and women
22:12		*anér*	Ananias, **a** devout **man** according to the law
23:1		*andres*	**Men** *and* brethren, I have lived in all good conscience
23:6		*andres*	**Men** *and* brethren, I am a Pharisee
23:21		*andres*	**men** who have bound themselves by an oath
23:27	*ton*	*andra*	This **man** was seized by the Jews
23:30	*ton*	*andra*	the Jews lay in wait for **the man**
24:5	*ton*	*andra*	we have found this **man** a plague
25:5	*tó*	*andri*	go down with *me* and accuse this **man**
25:14		*anér*	a certain **man** left a prisoner by Felix
25:17	*ton*	*andra*	commanded **the man** to be brought in
25:23	*tois*	*andrasin*	**the** prominent **men** of the city
25:24	*hoi*	*andres*	King Agrippa and all **the men** who are here
27:10		*andres*	**Men**, I perceive that this voyage will end
27:21		*andres*	**Men**, you should have listened to me
27:25		*andres*	take heart, **men**, for I believe God
28:17		*andres*	**Men** *and* brethren, though I have done nothing
Romans 4:8		*anér*	*Blessed is* **the man** *to whom the* LORD
7:2	*tó*	*andri*	bound by the law to *her* **husband**
7:2	*ho*	*anér*	But if **the husband** dies
7:2	*tou*	*andros*	released from the law of *her* **husband**

284

	7:3	tou	andros	if, while *her* **husband** lives
	7:3		andri	she marries another **man**
	7:3	ho	anér	but if her **husband** dies
	7:3		andri	though she has married another **man**
	11:4		andras	*for Myself seven thousand men*
1 Corinthians	7:2	ton	andra	each woman have her own **husband**
	7:3	ho	anér	Let **the husband** render to his wife
	7:3	tó	andri	likewise also the wife **to** her **husband**
	7:4	ho	anér	her own body, but **the husband**
	7:4	ho	anér	likewise **the husband** does not have authority
	7:10		andros	A wife is not to depart from *her* **husband**
	7:11	tó	andri	or be reconciled **to** *her* **husband**
	7:11		andra	**a husband** is not to divorce *his* wife
	7:13		andra	a woman who has **a husband**
	7:14	ho	anér	**the** unbelieving **husband** is sanctified
	7:14	tó	andri	the unbelieving wife is sanctified by **the husband**
	7:16	ton	andra	you will save *your* **husband**
	7:16		anér	how do you know, O **husband**, whether
	7:34	tó	andri	how she may please *her* **husband**
	7:39	ho	anér	as long as her **husband** lives
	7:39	ho	anér	but if her **husband** dies
	11:3		andros	the head of every **man** is Christ
	11:3	ho	anér	the head of woman *is* **man**
	11:4		anér	Every **man** praying or prophesying
	11:7		anér	**a man** indeed ought not to
	11:7		andros	woman is the glory **of man**
	11:8		anér	For **man** is not from woman
	11:8		andros	but woman from **man**

	11:9		*anér*	Nor was **man** created for the woman
	11:9	*ton*	*andra*	but woman for **the man**
	11:11		*anér*	neither *is* **man** independent of woman
	11:11		*andros*	nor woman independent **of man**
	11:12	*tou*	*andros*	for as the woman *was* from **the man**
	11:12	*ho*	*anér*	so **the man** also *is* through the woman
	11:14		*anér*	if **a man** has long hair
	13:11		*anér*	but when I became **a man**
	14:35	*tous*	*andras*	let them ask their own **husbands** at home
2 Corinthians	11:2		*andri*	betrothed you to one **husband**
Galatians	4:27	*ton*	*andra*	*Than she who has **a husband***
Ephesians	4:13		*andra*	to **a** perfect **man**
	5:22	*tois*	*andrasin*	submit to your own **husbands**
	5:23	*ho*	*anér*	**the husband** is head of the wife
	5:24	*tois*	*andrasin*	to their own **husbands** in everything
	5:25	*hoi*	*andres*	**Husbands,** love your wives
	5:28	*hoi*	*andres*	So **husbands** ought to love
	5:33	*ton*	*andra*	that she respects *her* **husband**
Colossians	3:18	*tois*	*andrasin*	Wives, submit to your own **husbands**
	3:19	*hoi*	*andres*	**Husbands,** love your wives
1 Timothy	2:8	*tous*	*andras*	I desire that **the men** pray
	2:12		*andros*	to have authority over **a man**
	3:2		*andra*	**the husband** of one wife
	3:12		*andres*	be **the husbands** of one wife
	5:9		*andros*	she has been the wife **of** one **man**
Titus	1:6		*anér*	**the husband** of one wife
	(2:4	*philandrous*		the young women to love their husbands)
	2:5	*tois*	*andrasin*	obedient to their own **husbands**
James	1:8		*anér*	**a** double-minded **man**, unstable
	1:12		*anér*	Blessed *is* **the man** who endures temptation

	1:20		*andros*	the wrath **of man** does not produce
	1:23		*andri*	he is like **a man** observing
	2:2		*anér*	into your assembly **a man** with gold
	3:2		*anér*	he *is* a perfect **man**, able
1 Peter	3:1	*tois*	*andrasin*	submissive **to** your own **husbands**
	3:5	*tois*	*andrasin*	being submissive **to** their own **husbands**
	3:7	*hoi*	*andres*	Likewise, *you* **husbands**, dwell with *them*
Revelation	21:2	*tó*	*andri*	as a bride adorned **for** her **husband**

Anér in it's Genitive form *andros*, or *andròn* in the plural

Within the midst of text of Chapter 9 a full breakdown of every verse where *anér* is found in the Genitive singular is given as it is found making use of the simple Genitive (it's basic normal sense). Here I give all the other places where *anér* is found in the Genitive starting with the basic use as before, but in the plural, then I give all the other uses of the Genitive of *anér* and it's uses in the New Testament.

Andròn this is *anér* in the plural Genitive

... 'For I say to you that none **of** those **men** who were invited shall taste my supper.'   *Luke 14:24*

*Legó - gar - humin, * hoti - oudeis - **tón - andrón** - ekeinón - tón - keklémenón - geusetai - mou - tou - deipnou.*

I say - for – to/for you (pl.) * since – no one - **of the – (of) men** - those – the [i.e. who] – have been invited – shall taste – of me/my – of the – (of) supper.

* * *

287

... "Therefore, **of** these **men** who have accompanied us all the time that the Lord Jesus went in and out among us,
Acts 1:21

*Dei - oun - **tón** - sunelthontón - hémin - **andrón** - en - panti - chronó - en - hó - eisélthen - kai - exélthen - eph' - hémas - ho - kurios - Iésous,*

It is necessary – therefore – **of the** – gathering/consorting – with us – **(of) men** – in – all – time – in – which – he came in – and – he went out – among – us – the – Lord – Jesus,

* * *

However, many of those who heard the word believed; and the number **of the men** came to be about five thousand.
Acts 4:4

*Polloi - de - tón - akousantón - ton - logon - episteusan, * kai - egenéthé - ho - arismos - **tón** - **andrón** - hósei - chiliades - pente.*

Many – but – of the – had heard – the – word – they believed, * and – became/it came to be – the – number – **of the** – **(of) men** – about – thousand – five.

* * *

And believers were increasingly added to the Lord, multitudes **of** both **men** and women,   *Acts 5:14*

... *mallon - de - prosetithento - pisteuontes - tó - kurió, * pléthé - **andrón** - te - kai - gunaikón.*

... more – and/but – were added – believers – to the/for the – (to/for) Lord, * multitudes – **of men** – (both) – and – of women;

* * *

288

"For some time ago Theudas rose up, claiming to be somebody. A number **of men**, about four hundred, joined him. He was slain, and all who obeyed him were scattered and came to nothing.   *Acts 5:36*

*Pro - gar - toutón - tón - hémerón - anesté - THeudas, * legón - einai - tina - heauton, * hó - prosekolléthé - arithmos - **andrón**, * hósei - tetrakosión. * hos - anérethé, * kai - pantes - hosoi - epeithonto - autó - dieluthésan - kai - egenonto - eis - ouden.*

Before – for – these – the – days – rose up – Theudas, * saying – to be – someone – himself, * to whom/ for whom – (they) were joined – a number – **of men**, * about – four hundred; * who – was put to death, * and – all – as many as – (they) were persuaded – by him – (they) were dispersed – and – came – to – nothing.

* * *

Therefore many of them believed, and also not a few of the Greeks, prominent women as well as **men**.   *Acts 17:12*

*Polloi - men - oun - ex - autón - episteusan, * kai - tón - HEllénidón - gunaikón - tón - euschémonón - kai - **andrón** - ouk - oligoi.*

Many – (indeed) – therefore – out of/from – them – (they) believed, * and – of the – (of) Greek – (of) women – of the – (of) honourable – and – **of men** – not – a few.

Those were the 6 places where "of a man" or, "of a husband" was found in the plural of *anér* as *andrón*. The other use of the Plural Genitive of *anér* (*andrón*) is as follows:

The queen of the South will rise up in the judgment with **the men** of this generation and condemn them, for she came

from the ends of the earth to hear the wisdom of Solomon;
and indeed a greater than Solomon *is* here.   *Luke 11:31*

Basilissa - notou - egerthésetai - en - té - krisei - meta -
***tón - andrón** - tés - geneas - tautés, * kai - katakrinei -*
autous. * hoti - hélthen - ek - tón - peratón - tés - gés -
akousai - tén - sophian - Solomóntos, * kai - idou,
* pleion - Solomóntos - hóde.

(A) queen – of [the] south – (she) shall rise up – in – the
– judging – with – **the** – **men** – of the – (of) generation
– this, * and – (she) shall condemn – them; * since – she
came – out of/from – the – ends – of the – (of) earth – to
hear – the – wisdom – of Solomon, * and – look, * (a)
more – of Solomon - here.

Here the Genitive is used to denote whether *meta* means "with" or
"after". When the word *meta* is followed by the Genitive it means
"with" (plural: *meta tón andrón* = with the men or, singular: *meta
tou andros* = with the man) ; when it is followed by the Accusative it
means "after" (plural: *meta tous andras* = after the men or, singular:
meta ton andra = after the man). Now follows the other uses of the
singular Genitive of *anér* (*andros*):

Whoever divorces his wife and marries another commits
adultery; and whoever marries her who is divorced from *her*
husband commits adultery.   *Luke 16:18*

Pas - ho - apoluón - tén - gunaika - autou - kai -
gamón - heteran - moicheuei. * kai - pas - ho - apolelu-
menén - apo - ***andros** - gamón - moicheuei.*

Every/All – the (one) – puts away – the – wife – of his –
and – marries – (an)other – he commits adultery; * and
– all/everyone – the (one) – put away – from – **a husband**
– marries – he commits adultery.

Here was the use of the Genetive following the word *apo* which
means "from": *apo an*dros = from a man/a husband. Both the word

290

ek = out of/from and *apo* are always followed by the genitive: the ablative or separation use of the Genitive.

> Now there was one, Anna, a prophetess, the daughter of Phanuel, of the tribe of Asher. She was of a great age, and had lived with **a husband** seven years from her virginity . . .
>
> *Luke 2:36*

> *Kai - bén - Anna - prophétis, * thugatér - PHanouél, * ek - phulés - Asér. * hauté - probebékuia - en - hémerais - pollais, * zésasa - eté - meta - **andros** - epta - apo - tés - parthenias - autés,*

> And – (she) was – Anna – a prophetess, * daughter - (of) Phanuel, * out of/from – tribe – (of) Asher; * she – advanced – in – days – many * (having) lived – years – with – **a husband** – seven – from – the – virginity – of her,

That was as the above last example of the plural given, *meta* followed by the Genitive means "with". *Meta andros* = with a husband.

> Then Ananias answered, 'Lord, I have heard from many about this **man**, how much harm he has done to Your saints in Jerusalem.' *Acts 9:13*

> *Apekrithé - de - ho - Ananias, * Kurie, * akékoa - apo - pollón - peri - **tou** - **andros** - toutou, * hosa - kaka - epoiésen - tois - hagiois - sou - en - HIerousalém.*

> Answered – but/and – the – Ananias, * Lord, * I have heard – from – many – about – **the** – **man** – this, * how much – evils/'bads' – he did – to the/ for the – (to/for) saints – of You – in – Jerusalem;

Here the Genitive follows the word *peri* and means "concerning" (i.e. "about such and such . . ."). Followed by the Accusative *peri* means "approximately" or, "(a-)round". It is the word from which we obtain periphery or peripheral i.e. around. It refers to a "circular" thought.

So then if, **while** *her* **husband** lives, she marries another man, she will be called an adulteress; but if her husband dies, she is free from that law, so that she is no adulteress, though she has married another man.   *Romans 7:3*

*Ara - oun - zóntos - **tou** - **andros** - moichalis - chrématisei, * ean - genétai - andri - heteró. * ean - de - apothané - ho - anér, * eleuthera - estin - apo - tou - nomou, * tou - mé - einai - autén - moichalida, * genomenén - andri - eteró.*

So – therefore – living – **while/during** which the – **husband** – (an) adulteress – (she) shall be called, * if - she be – to a man/ for a man – (to/for) another; * if – but – should die – the – husband, * free – she is – from – the – law, * of the [law] – not – to be – her – an adulteress, * (having) become – to/for a man – another.

The use of the Genitive above is in it's role as "the time during which".

For man is not from woman, but woman from **man**.

1 Corinthians 11:8

*. . . ou - gar - estin - anér - ek - gunaikos, * alla - guné - ex - **andros**.*

. . . not – for – he is – a man – out of/from – a woman, * but – a – woman – out of/from – **a man**;

Here the preposition *ek* is seen. It is always followed by the Genitive. *Ek* means "out of" or, "from" (as in "from the source" as opposed to "away from"). Before a vowel *ek* contracts to *ex*.

Nevertheless, neither *is* man independent of woman, nor woman independent of **man**, in the Lord.

1 Corinthians 11:11

*Plén - oute - anér - chóris - gunaikos, * oute - guné - chóris - **andros**, * en - kurió.*

However – neither/nor – a man – apart from – a woman, *
nor/neither – a woman – apart from – **a man**, * in – Lord;

This is an example of the preposition *chóris* which means "apart from". It is always followed by the Genitive.

APPENDIX 5

✧

ANTHRÓPOS

Here follows the word *anthrópos* in all its forms in the New Testament.

This is useful to help show two things. First that since *anér* is recognised as representing either a particular man or, a husband, *anthrópos* instead is the word which best represents "someone" or "a person" and is thus used to denote things referring to men and women in general. So much so that in the plural it is used to refer basically to a group of people which would include women.

Second this word which represents the race of man as opposed to a particular man explicitly is often used by Jesus used when He called Himself the Son of Man, His favourite title.

The reference is first given in the order as found in the New Testament. Then the word *anthrópos* in the declension used in the Greek passage. Then the translation in English as found in the NKJV.

N.B. As mentioned in the preface: notes to the book, I use the letter "e" with the acute accent "é" to denote the Greek letter "heta" (the long "e") to differentiate from "epsilon". Similarly I use the letter "o" with the acute accent "ó" to denote the Greek letter "omega" (the long "o") to differentiate from "omicron".

The declensions of *anthrópos* preceded by those of the definite article (male only)
A declension is the name for the different beginnings and mostly endings of a word to show its relationship with other words in a sentence. The example in English that remains is the genitive case – the name for the relationship of belonging to or, being offspring of. Example: a man's son: where " 's" is the declension of man.

You may also notice that in highlighting in bold the English translation I also highlight the indefinite article "a". There is no separate word in Greek for "a" and whenever the definite article is not present this is taken by translators from anthrópos itself.

The *ho*	Nominative	singular	*anthrópos*	**man**
hoi	(the subject)	plural	*anthrópoi*	**men/peoples**
ton	Accusative	singular	*anthrópon*	
tous	(the direct object)	plural	*anthrópous*	
tó	Dative	singular	*anthrópó*	
tois	(the indirect object)	plural	*anthrópois*	
	for a man – to a man			
tou	Genitive	singular	*anthrópou*	
tón	(the belonging to)	plural	*anthrópón*	
	of a man – a man's			
n/a	Vocative	singular	*anthrópe*	
n/a	(the spoken)	plural	n/a	

Passages of the New Testament with *anthrópos*
The Received Text is used throughout

ho huios tou anthrópou - the Son of Man - literally, "the son of (the) man"

For interest and aesthetics (so it looks good) ***tou anthrópou* – and Son of Man** have been highlighted. You may notice that "the" in front of "Son of Man" is not highlighted in the English whilst "*tou*" is in the Greek. This is because the definite article in the English is the translation of "the Son" and not "of the Man". The definite article "the" thus repeated is not normally translated, but "dropped". By this name Jesus called Himself more that any other. It occurs 86 times in the New Testament and was also the name given prophetically of the Lord in the book of Enoch before that. Not such a well known apocryphal book, but is alluded to by Peter and Jesus and directly quoted by Jude:

Now Enoch, the seventh from Adam, prophesied about these men also saying, "Behold, the Lord comes with ten thousands of His saints, to execute judgment on all to convict all, who are ungodly among them of all their ungodly deeds which they have committed in an ungodly way, and of all the harsh things which ungodly sinners have spoken against Him."   *Jude 14-15*

Matthew	4:4		*anthrópos*	It is written, '*Man shall not live by bread*
	4:19		*anthrópón*	I will make you fishers of men
	5:13	*tón*	*anthrópón*	thrown out and trampled underfoot by men
	5:16	*tón*	*anthrópón*	Let your light so shine before men
	5:19	*tous*	*anthrópous*	these commandments, and teaches men so
	6:1	*tón*	*anthrópón*	do your charitable deeds before men
	6:2	*tón*	*anthrópón*	that they may have glory from men
	6:5	*tois*	*anthrópois*	that they may be seen by men
	6:14	*tois*	*anthrópois*	For if you forgive men their trespasses
	6:15	*tois*	*anthrópois*	But if you do not forgive men their trespasses
	6:16	*tois*	*anthrópois*	that they may appear to men to be fasting
	6:18	*tois*	*anthrópois*	do not appear to men to be fasting
	7:9		*anthrópos*	Or what man is there among you
	7:12	*hoi*	*anthrópoi*	whatever you want men to do to you
	8:9		*anthrópos*	For I also am a man under authority
	8:20	*tou*	*anthrópou*	but **the Son of Man** has nowhere to lay

8:27	*hoi*	*anthrópoi*	And the men marvelled, saying, "Who can this be
9:6	*tou*	*anthrópou*	that you may know **the Son of Man** has power
9:8	*tois*	*anthrópois*	who had given such power to men
9:9		*anthrópon*	He saw a man named Matthew sitting
9:32		*anthrópon*	they brought to Him a man, mute
10:17	*tón*	*anthrópón*	But beware of men, for they will deliver you up
10:23	*tou*	*anthrópou*	the cities of Israel before **the Son of Man** comes
10:32	*tón*	*anthrópón*	Therefore whoever confesses Me before men
10:33	*tón*	*anthrópón*	But whoever denies Me before men, him
10:35		*anthrópon*	come to '*set a man against his father*
10:36	*tou*	*anthrópou*	And '*a man's foes will be those of his own*
11:8		*anthrópon*	go out to see? a man clothed in soft garments
11:19	*tou*	*anthrópou*	**The Son of Man** came eating and drinking
11:19		*anthrópos*	they say, 'Look, a gluttonous man
12:8	*tou*	*anthrópou*	For **the Son of Man** is Lord even of the Sabbath
12:10		*anthrópos*	behold, there was a man who had a withered
12:11		*anthrópos*	What man is there among you who has one sheep
12:12		*anthrópos*	much more value then is a man than a sheep
12:13	*tó*	*anthrópó*	He said to the man, "Stretch out your hand."

12:31	*tois*	*anthrópois*	every sin and blasphemy will be forgiven men
12:31	*tois*	*anthrópois*	*against* the Spirit will not be forgiven men
12:32	*tou*	*anthrópou*	speaks a word against **the Son of Man**
12:35	*ho*	*anthrópos*	A good man out of the good treasure of
12:35	*ho*	*anthrópos*	an evil man out of the evil treasure
12:36	*hoi*	*anthrópoi*	for every idle word men may
12:40	*tou*	*anthrópou*	so will **the Son of Man** be three days
12:43	*tou*	*anthrópou*	unclean spirit goes out of a man
12:45	*tou*	*anthrópou*	and the last *state* of that man is worse
13:24		*anthrópó*	kingdom of heaven is like a man who sowed
13:25	*tous*	*anthrópous*	but while men slept, his enemy came
13:31		*anthrópos*	a mustard seed, which a man took
13:37	*tou*	*anthrópou*	He who sows the good seed is **the Son of Man**
13:41	*tou*	*anthrópou*	**The Son of Man** will send out His angels
13:44		*anthrópos*	treasure hidden in a field, which a man found
13:45		*anthrópó*	kingdom of heaven is like a merchant seeking [the kingdom of heaven is like a merchant man, seeking goodly pearls KJV]
13:52		*anthrópó*	kingdom of heaven is like a householder [the kingdom of heaven is like unto a man *that is* an

			householder, which bringeth KJV]
15:9		*anthrópón*	*Teaching as doctrines the commandments of men*
15:11	*ton*	*anthrópon*	Not what goes into the mouth defiles a man
15:11	*ton*	*anthrópon*	comes out of the mouth, this defiles a man
15:18	*ton*	*anthrópon*	come from the heart, and they defile a man
15:20	*ton*	*anthrópon*	These are *the things* which defile a man
15:20	*ton*	*anthrópon*	unwashed hands does not defile a man
16:13	*hoi*	*anthrópoi*	asked His disciples, saying, "Who do men say
16:13	*tou*	*anthrópou*	say that I, **the Son of Man**, am?
16:23	*tón*	*anthrópón*	the things of God, but the things of men
16:26		*anthrópos*	For what is a man profited if he gains the whole
16:26		*anthrópos*	what will a man give in exchange for his soul
16:27	*tou*	*anthrópou*	For **the Son of Man** will come in the glory of
16:28	*tou*	*anthrópou*	taste death till they see **the Son of Man** coming
17:9	*tou*	*anthrópou*	the vision to no one until **the Son of Man** is risen
17:12	*tou*	*anthrópou*	Likewise **the Son of Man** is also about to suffer
17:14		*anthrópos*	a man came to Him, kneeling down to Him
17:22	*tou*	*anthrópou*	said to them, "**The Son of Man** is about to be
17:22		*anthrópón*	betrayed into the hands of men
18:7	*tó*	*anthrópó*	woe to that man by whom the offence comes!

18:11	*tou*	*anthrópou*	For **the Son of Man** has come to save
18:12		*anthrópó*	If a man has a hundred sheep, and one of them
19:3		*anthrópó*	Is it lawful for a man to divorce his wife
19:5		*anthrópos*	*For this reason a man shall leave his father*
19:6		*anthrópos*	God has joined together, let not man separate
19:10	*tou*	*anthrópou*	such is the case of the man with *his* wife
19:12	*tón*	*anthrópón*	eunuchs who were made eunuchs by men
19:26		*anthrópois*	said to them, "With men this is impossible
19:28	*tou*	*anthrópou*	in the regeneration, when **the Son of Man** sits
20:1		*anthrópó*	kingdom of heaven is like a landowner who [the kingdom of heaven is like unto a man *that is* an householder, which went out early KJV]
20:18	*tou*	*anthrópou*	**the Son of Man** will be betrayed to
20:28	*tou*	*anthrópou*	**the Son of Man** did not come to be served
21:25		*anthrópón*	was it from? From heaven or from men?
21:26		*anthrópón*	if we say, 'From men,' we fear the multitude
21:28		*anthrópos*	A man had two sons, and he came to the first
22:11		*anthrópon*	he saw a man there who did not have
22:16		*anthrópón*	You do not regard the person of men
23:4	*tón*	*anthrópón*	to bear, and lay *them* on men's shoulders

23:5	*tois*	*anthrópois*	works they do to be seen by men
23:7	*tón*	*anthrópón*	and to be called by men, 'Rabbi, Rabbi.'
(23:14) 23:13	*tón*	*anthrópón*	you shut up the kingdom of heaven against men
23:28	*tois*	*anthrópois*	outwardly appear righteous to men, but inside
24:27	*tou*	*anthrópou*	so also will the coming of **the Son of Man** be
24:30	*tou*	*anthrópou*	the sign of **the Son of Man** will appear in heaven
24:30	*tou*	*anthrópou*	they will see **the Son of Man** coming on the clouds
24:37	*tou*	*anthrópou*	so also will the coming of **the Son of Man** be
24:39	*tou*	*anthrópou*	so also will the coming of **the Son of Man** be
24:44	*tou*	*anthrópou*	for **the Son of Man** is coming at an hour when
25:13	*tou*	*anthrópou*	nor the hour in which **the Son of Man** is coming
25:14		*anthrópos*	like a man travelling to a far country
25:24		*anthrópos*	I knew you to be a hard man, reaping where
25:31	*tou*	*anthrópou*	When **the Son of Man** comes in His glory
26:2	*tou*	*anthrópou*	and **the Son of Man** will be delivered up to be
26:24	*tou*	*anthrópou*	**The Son of Man** goes as it is written of Him
26:24	*tó*	*anthrópó*	woe to that man by whom the
26:24	*tou*	*anthrópou*	by whom **the Son of Man** is betrayed!
26:45	*tou*	*anthrópou*	at hand, and **the Son of Man** is being betrayed
26:64	*tou*	*anthrópou*	hereafter you will see **the Son of Man** sitting

26:72	*ton*	*anthrópon*	with an oath, "I do not know the Man!"
26:74	*ton*	*anthrópon*	swear, *saying*, "I do not know the Man!"
27:32		*anthrópon*	they found a man of Cyrene, Simon by name
27:57		*anthrópos*	there came a rich man from Arimathea

Mark

1:17		*anthrópón*	make you become fishers of men
1:23		*anthrópos*	Now there was a man in their synagogue
2:10	*tou*	*anthrópou*	that you may know that **the Son of Man** has power
2:27	*ton*	*anthrópon*	to them, "The Sabbath was made for man,
2:27	*ho*	*anthrópos*	and not man for the Sabbath.
2:28	*tou*	*anthrópou*	**the Son of Man** is also Lord of the Sabbath
3:1		*anthrópos*	and a man was there who had a withered hand
3:3	*tó*	*anthrópó*	He said to the man who had the withered hand
3:5	*tó*	*anthrópó*	He said to the man, "Stretch out your hand."
3:28	*tón*	*anthrópón*	sins will be forgiven the sons of men, and
4:26		*anthrópos*	as if a man should scatter seed on the ground
5:2		*anthrópos*	out of the tombs a man with an unclean spirit
5:8	*tou*	*anthrópou*	said to him, "Come out of the man, unclean spirit!"
7:7		*anthrópón*	*Teaching as doctrines the commandments of men*
7:8	*tón*	*anthrópón*	you hold the tradition of men – the washing of
7:11		*anthrópos*	If a man says to his father or mother

7:15	*tou*	*anthrópou*	nothing that enters a man from outside
7:15	*ton*	*anthrópon*	those are the things that defile a man
7:18	*ton*	*anthrópon*	whatever enters a man from outside cannot
7:20	*tou*	*anthrópou*	He said, "What comes out of a man,
7:20	*ton*	*anthrópon*	that defiles a man."
7:21	*tón*	*anthrópón*	from within, out of the heart of men, proceed
7:23	*ton*	*anthrópon*	come from within and defile a man
8:24	*tous*	*anthrópous*	I see men like trees, walking
8:27	*hoi*	*anthrópoi*	saying to them, "Who do men say that I am?"
8:31	*tou*	*anthrópou*	that **the Son of Man** must suffer many
8:33	*tón*	*anthrópón*	of the things of God, but the things of men
8:36		*anthrópon*	what will it profit a man if he gains
8:37		*anthrópos*	what will a man give in exchange for his soul
8:38	*tou*	*anthrópou*	**the Son of Man** also will be ashamed when He
9:9	*tou*	*anthrópou*	till **the Son of Man** had risen from the dead
9:12	*tou*	*anthrópou*	concerning **the Son of Man**, that He must suffer
9:31	*tou*	*anthrópou*	said to them, "**The Son of Man** is being
9:31		*anthrópón*	delivered into the hands of men, and they
10:7		*anthrópos*	*For this reason a man shall leave his father*
10:9		*anthrópos*	joined together, let no man separate

10:27		*anthrópois*	Jesus said, "With men *it is* impossible
10:33	*tou*	*anthrópou*	and **the Son of Man** will be delivered to the chief
10:45	*tou*	*anthrópou*	even **the Son of Man** did not come to be served
11:2		*anthrópón*	a colt tied, on which no one sat
			[ye shall find a colt tied, whereon never man sat; loose him, and bring *him* KJV]
11:30		*anthrópón*	was it from heaven or from men? Answer Me
11:32		*anthrópón*	if we say, 'From men'"- they feared the people
12:1		*anthrópos*	a man planted a vineyard and set a hedge
12:14		*anthrópón*	You do not regard the person of men, but teach
13:26	*tou*	*anthrópou*	they will see **the Son of Man** coming in the clouds
13:34		*anthrópos*	*It is* like a man going to a far country
14:13		*anthrópos*	Go into the city, and a man will meet you
14:21	*tou*	*anthrópou*	**The Son of Man** indeed goes just as it is written of Him, but woe to that man by whom
14:21	*tó*	*anthrópó*	of Him, but woe to that man by whom
14:21	*tou*	*anthrópou*	**the Son of Man** is betrayed! It would have
14:21	*ho*	*anthrópos*	have been good for that man if he had never
14:41	*tou*	*anthrópou*	behold, **the Son of Man** is being betrayed into
14:62	*tou*	*anthrópou*	you will see **the Son of Man** sitting at the right hand

	14:71	*ton*	*anthrópon*	I do not know this Man of whom you speak!
	15:39	*ho*	*anthrópos*	Truly this Man was the Son of God!
Luke	1:25		*anthrópois*	to take away my reproach among men
	2:14		*anthrópois*	on earth peace, good will toward men!
	2:25		*anthrópos*	behold, there was a man in Jerusalem whose
	2:25	*ho*	*anthrópos*	name was Simeon, and this man was just
	2:52		*anthrópois*	and stature, and in favour with God and men
	4:4	*ho*	*anthrópos*	It is written, '*Man shall not live by bread alone*
	4:33		*anthrópos*	in the synagogue there was a man who had a spirit
	5:10		*anthrópous*	From now on you will catch men
	5:18		*anthrópon*	brought on a bed a man who was paralyzed
	5:20		*anthrópe*	He said to him, "Man your sins are forgiven you."
	5:24	*tou*	*anthrópou*	you may know that **the Son of Man** has power
	6:5	*tou*	*anthrópou*	**The Son of Man** is also Lord of the Sabbath
	6:6		*anthrópos*	And a man was there whose hand was withered
	6:8	*tó*	*anthrópó*	and said to the man who had the withered hand
	6:10	*tó*	*anthrópó*	He said to the man, "Stretch out your hand."
	6:22	*hoi*	*anthrópoi*	Blessed are you when men hate you
	6:22	*tou*	*anthrópou*	your name evil, for **the Son of Man**'s sake
	6:26	*hoi*	*anthrópoi*	Woe to you when all men speak well of you

306

6:31	hoi	anthrópoi	just as you want men to do to you
6:45	ho	anthrópos	A good man out of the good treasure of his heart
6:45	ho	anthrópos	an evil man out of the evil treasure of his heart
6:48		anthrópó	He is like a man building a house
6:49		anthrópó	like a man who built a house on the earth
7:8		anthrópos	For I also am a man placed under authority
7:25		anthrópon	A man clothed in soft garments?
7:31	tous	anthrópous	To what then shall I liken the men of this generation
7:34	**tou**	**anthrópou**	**The Son of Man** has come eating and drinking
7:34		anthrópos	and you say, 'Look, a glutton and a wine-bibber [and ye say, Behold a gluttonous man, and a wine-bibber, a friend of publicans and sinners KJV]
8:29	tou	anthrópou	the unclean spirit to come out of the man
8:33	tou	anthrópou	the demons went out of the man and entered the
8:35	ton	anthrópon	came to Jesus, and found the man from whom
9:22	**tou**	**anthrópou**	**The Son of Man** must suffer many things
9:25		anthrópos	what advantage is it to a man if he gains
9:26	**tou**	**anthrópou**	of him **the Son of Man** will be ashamed when
9:44	**tou**	**anthrópou**	for **the Son of Man** is about to be
9:44		anthrópón	delivered into the hands of men

9:56	*tou*	*anthrópou*	For the Son of Man did not come to
9:56		*anthrópón*	destroy men's lives but to save *them*
9:58	*tou*	*anthrópou*	the Son of Man has nowhere to lay His head
10:30		*anthrópos*	A certain man went down from Jerusalem to Jericho
11:24	*tou*	*anthrópou*	When an unclean spirit goes out of a man
11:26	*tou*	*anthrópou*	the last *state* of that man is worse than the first
11:30	*tou*	*anthrópou*	so also the Son of Man will be to this generation
11:44	*hoi*	*anthrópoi*	and the men who walk over *them* are not aware
11:46	*tous*	*anthrópous*	you load men with burdens hard to bear
12:8	*tón*	*anthrópón*	whoever confesses Me before men
12:8	*tou*	*anthrópou*	him the Son of Man also will confess before
12:9	*tón*	*anthrópón*	he who denies Me before men will be denied
12:10	*tou*	*anthrópou*	a word against the Son of Man, it will be
12:14		*anthrópe*	He said to him, "Man, who made Me a judge
12:16		*anthrópou*	The ground of a certain rich man yielded plentifully
12:36		*anthrópois*	you yourselves be like men who wait for their master
12:40	*tou*	*anthrópou*	you also be ready, for the Son of Man is coming
13:4		*anthrópous*	worse sinners than all *other* men who dwelt in
13:19		*anthrópos*	like a mustard seed, which a man took and put
14:2		*anthrópos*	there was a certain man before Him who had

14:16		*anthrópos*	A certain man gave a great supper and invited many
14:30	*ho*	*anthrópos*	This man began to build and was not able to finish
15:4		*anthrópos*	What man of you, having a hundred sheep
15:11		*anthrópos*	He said: "A certain man had two sons.
16:1		*anthrópos*	There was a certain rich man who had a steward
16:15	*tón*	*anthrópón*	justify yourselves before men, but God knows
16:15		*anthrópois*	what is highly esteemed among men is an
16:19		*anthrópos*	a certain rich man who was clothed in purple
17:22	**tou**	**anthrópou**	one of the days of **the Son of Man**
17:24	**tou**	**anthrópou**	so also **the Son of Man** will be in His day
17:26	**tou**	**anthrópou**	so it will be also in the days of **the Son of Man**
17:30	**tou**	**anthrópou**	in the day when **the Son of Man** is revealed
18:2		*anthrópon*	a judge who did not fear God nor regard man
18:4		*anthrópon*	Though I do not fear God nor regard man
18:8	**tou**	**anthrópou**	when **the Son of Man** comes, will he really
18:10		*anthrópoi*	Two men went up to the temple to pray
18:11	*tón*	*anthrópón*	I thank you that I am not like other men
18:27		*anthrópois*	impossible with men are possible with God
18:31	**tou**	**anthrópou**	concerning **the Son of Man** will be accomplished
19:10	**tou**	**anthrópou**	**the Son of Man** has come to seek and to save

19:21		*anthrópos*	I feared you, because you are an austere man
19:22		*anthrópos*	You knew that I was an austere man
19:30		*anthrópón*	a colt tied, on which no one has ever sat [ye shall find a colt tied, whereon yet never man sat: loose him KJV]
20:4		*anthrópón*	was it from heaven or from men?
20:6		*anthrópón*	if we say, 'From men,' all the people will stone us
20:9		*anthrópos*	A certain man planted a vineyard, leased it
21:26		*anthrópón*	men's hearts failing them from fear
21:27	*tou*	*anthrópou*	they will see **the Son of Man** coming in a cloud
21:36	*tou*	*anthrópou*	and to stand before **the Son of Man**
22:10		*anthrópos*	entered the city, a man will meet you carrying
22:22	*tou*	*anthrópou*	And truly **the Son of Man** goes as it has been
22:22	*tó*	*anthrópó*	but woe to that man by whom He is betrayed!
22:48	*tou*	*anthrópou*	are you betraying **the Son of Man** with a kiss?
22:58		*anthrópe*	But Peter said, "Man, I am not!"
22:60		*anthrópe*	Man, I do not know what you are saying!
22:69	*tou*	*anthrópou*	Hereafter **the Son of Man** will sit on the right hand
23:4	*tó*	*anthrópó*	I find no fault in this Man
23:6	*ho*	*anthrópos*	he asked if the Man were a Galilean
23:14	*ton*	*anthrópon*	You have brought this Man to me, as one who

	23:14	*tó*	*anthrópó*	I have found no fault in this Man concerning
	23:47	*ho*	*anthrópos*	Certainly this was a righteous Man!
	24:7	**tou**	**anthrópou**	**The Son of Man** must be delivered into
	24:7		*anthrópón*	the hands of sinful men, and be crucified
John	1:4	*tón*	*anthrópón*	In Him was life, and the life was the light of men
	1:6		*anthrópos*	There was a man sent from God, whose name
	1:9		*anthrópon*	light to every man who comes into the world
	1:51	**tou**	**anthrópou**	ascending and descending upon **the Son of Man**
	2:10		*anthrópos*	Every man at the beginning sets out the good wine
	2:25	*tou*	*anthrópou*	need that anyone should testify of man
	2:25	*tó*	*anthrópó*	for He knew what was in man
	3:1		*anthrópos*	There was a man of the Pharisees named
	3:4		*anthrópos*	How can a man be born when he is old
	3:13	**tou**	**anthrópou**	**the Son of Man** who is in heaven
	3:14	**tou**	**anthrópou**	even so must **the Son of Man** be lifted up
	3:19	*hoi*	*anthrópoi*	and men loved darkness rather than light
	3:27		*anthrópos*	A man can receive nothing unless it has
	4:28	*tois*	*anthrópois*	went her way into the city, and said to the men
	4:29		*anthrópon*	Come, see a Man who told me all things
	4:50	*ho*	*anthrópos*	So the man believed the word that Jesus spoke

5:5		*anthrópos*	Now a certain man was there who had an
5:7		*anthrópon*	Sir, I have no man to put me into the pool
5:9	*ho*	*anthrópos*	And immediately the man was made well
5:12	*ho*	*anthrópos*	Who is the Man who said to you, "Take up your
5:15	*ho*	*anthrópos*	The man departed and told the Jews
5:27		***anthrópou***	judgment also, because He is **the Son of Man**
5:34		*anthrópou*	I do not receive testimony from man
5:41		*anthrópón*	I do not receive honour from men
6:10	*tous*	*anthrópous*	Jesus said, "Make the people sit down."
6:14	*hoi*	*anthrópoi*	Then those men, when they had seen the sign
6:27	*tou*	***anthrópou***	everlasting life, which **the Son of Man** will give you
6:53	*tou*	***anthrópou***	the flesh of **the Son of Man** and drink
6:62	*tou*	***anthrópou***	if you should see **the Son of Man** ascend where
7:22		*anthrópon*	and you circumcise a man on the Sabbath
7:23		*anthrópos*	If a man receives circumcision on the Sabbath
7:23		*anthrópon*	because I made a man completely well on
7:46		*anthrópos*	The officers answered, "No man
7:46	*ho*	*anthrópos*	ever spoke like this Man!"
7:51	*ton*	*anthrópon*	Does our law judge a man before it hears him
8:17		*anthrópón*	that the testimony of two men is true

8:28	*tou*	*anthrópou*	When you lift up **the Son of Man**, then you will
8:40		*anthrópon*	seek to kill Me, a Man who has told you the truth
9:1		*anthrópon*	He saw a man who was blind from birth
9:11		*anthrópos*	A man called Jesus made clay and anointed
9:16	*ho*	*anthrópos*	This Man is not from God, because He does not
9:16		*anthrópos*	How can a man who is a sinner do such signs
9:24	*ton*	*anthrópon*	they again called the man who was blind
9:24	*ho*	*anthrópos*	We know that this Man is a sinner
9:30	*ho*	*anthrópos*	The man answered and said to them
10:33		*anthrópos*	You, being a Man, make Yourself God
11:47	*ho*	*anthrópos*	For this Man works many signs
11:50		*anthrópos*	expedient for us that one man should die
12:23	*tou*	*anthrópou*	The hour has come that **the Son of Man** should
12:34	*tou*	*anthrópou*	**The Son of Man** must be lifted up
12:34	*tou*	*anthrópou*	Who is this **Son of Man**?
12:43	*tón*	*anthrópón*	loved the praise of men more than the praise
13:31	*tou*	*anthrópou*	Now **the Son of Man** is glorified, and God is
16:21		*anthrópos*	for joy that a human being has been born
17:6	*tois*	*anthrópois*	manifested Your name to the men whom You
18:14		*anthrópon*	expedient that one man should die for the people

	18:17	*tou*	*anthrópou*	are not also *one* of this Man's disciples, are you?
	18:29	*tou*	*anthrópou*	accusation do you bring against this Man?
	19:5	*ho*	*anthrópos*	said to them, "Behold the Man!"
Acts	4:9		*anthrópou*	good deed *done* to *the* helpless man
	4:12		*anthrópois*	given among men by which we must be saved
	4:13		*anthrópoi*	they were uneducated and untrained men
	4:14	*ton*	*anthrópon*	And seeing the man who had been healed
	4:16	*tois*	*anthrópois*	What shall we do to these men
	4:17		*anthrópón*	they speak to no man in this name
	4:22	*ho*	*anthrópos*	For the man was over forty years old
	5:4		*anthrópois*	You have not lied to men but to God
	5:28	*tou*	*anthrópou*	to bring this Man's blood on us
	5:29		*anthrópois*	We ought to obey God rather than men
	5:35	*tois*	*anthrópois*	you intend to do regarding these men
	5:38	*tón*	*anthrópón*	keep away from these men and let them alone
	5:38		*anthrópón*	for if this plan or this work is of men
	6:13	*ho*	*anthrópos*	This man does not cease to speak blasphemous
	7:56	*tou*	*anthrópou*	heavens opened and **the Son of Man** standing
	9:33		*anthrópon*	he found a certain man named Aeneas
	10:26		*anthrópos*	stand up; I myself am also a man

10:28		*anthrópon*	should not call any man common or unclean
12:22		*anthrópou*	The voice of a god and not of a man
14:11		*anthrópois*	down to us in the likeness of men
14:15		*anthrópoi*	We also are men with the same nature
15:17	*tón*	*anthrópón*	*that the rest of mankind may seek the LORD*
15:26		*anthrópois*	men who have risked their lives for the name
16:17	*hoi*	*anthrópoi*	These men are the servants of the Most High God
16:20	*hoi*	*anthrópoi*	These men, being Jews, exceedingly trouble
16:35	*tous*	*anthrópous*	saying, "Let those men go."
17:25		*anthrópón*	Nor is He worshipped with men's hands
17:26		*anthrópón*	from one blood every nation of men
17:29		*anthrópou*	something shaped by art and man's devising
17:30	*tois*	*anthrópois*	but now commands all men everywhere
18:13	*tous*	*anthrópous*	This *fellow* persuades men to worship God
19:16	*ho*	*anthrópos*	Then the man in whom the evil spirit was
19:35		*anthrópos*	what man is there who does not know that
21:28	*ho*	*anthrópos*	This is the man who teaches all *men* everywhere
21:39		*anthrópos*	But Paul said, "I am a Jew from Tarsus [But Paul said, I am a man *which am* a Jew of Tarsus, *a city* in Cilicia KJV]
22:15		*anthrópous*	you will be His witness to all men of what

22:25		*anthrópon*	to scourge a man who is a Roman
22:26	*ho*	*anthrópos*	Take care what you do, for this man is a Roman
23:9	*tó*	*anthrópó*	We find no evil in this man; but if a spirit or an angel
24:16	*tous*	*anthrópous*	a conscience without offense toward God and men
25:16		*anthrópon*	the Romans to deliver any man to destruction
25:22	*tou*	*anthrópou*	I also would like to hear the man myself
26:31	*ho*	*anthrópos*	This man is doing nothing worthy of death or chains
26:32	*ho*	*anthrópos*	This man might have been set free if he had not
28:4	*ho*	*anthrópos*	No doubt this man is a murderer, whom, though
Romans 1:18		*anthrópón*	unrighteousness of men, who suppress the truth
1:23		*anthrópou*	an image made like corruptible man
2:1		*anthrópe*	you are inexcusable, O man, whoever you are
2:3		*anthrópe*	O man, you who judge those practising such
2:9		*anthrópou*	on every soul of man who does evil
2:16	*tón*	*anthrópón*	judge the secrets of men by Jesus Christ
2:29		*anthrópón*	whose praise *is* not from men but from God
3:4		*anthrópos*	let God be true but every man a liar
3:5		*anthrópon*	who inflicts wrath? (I speak as a man.)
3:28		*anthrópon*	a man is justified by faith apart from

4:6	*tou*	*anthrópou*	the blessedness of the man to whom God imputes
5:12		*anthrópou*	through one man sin entered the world
5:12		*anthrópous*	thus death spread to all men, because
5:15	*tou*	*anthrópou*	by the grace of the one Man, Jesus Christ
5:18		*anthrópous*	came to all men, resulting in condemnation
5:18		*anthrópous*	*came* to all men resulting in justification
5:19		*anthrópou*	For as by one man's disobedience many
6:6		*anthrópos*	our old man was crucified with *Him*
7:1	*tou*	*anthrópou*	the law has dominion over a man as long as he lives
7:22	*ton*	*anthrópon*	the law of God according to the inward man
7:24		*anthrópos*	O wretched man that I am! Who will deliver
9:20		*anthrópe*	But indeed, O man, who are you to reply against
10:5		*anthrópos*	*The man who does these things shall live by them*
12:17		*anthrópón*	regard for good things in the sight of all men
12:18		*anthrópón*	live peaceably with all men
14:18	*tois*	*anthrópois*	acceptable to God and approved by men
14:20	*tó*	*anthrópó*	*it is* evil for the man who eats with offense
1 Corinthians 1:25	*tón*	*anthrópón*	foolishness of God is wiser than men
1:25	*tón*	*anthrópón*	weakness of God is stronger than men
2:5		*anthrópón*	in the wisdom of men but in the power of God

2:9		*anthrópou*	nor have entered into the heart of man
2:11		*anthrópón*	For what man knows the things
2:11	*tou*	*anthrópou*	of a man except the spirit
2:11	*tou*	*anthrópou*	of the man which is in him?
2:14		*anthrópos*	But the natural man does not receive
3:3		*anthrópon*	are you not carnal and behaving like *mere* men?
3:21		*anthrópois*	Therefore let no one glory in men
4:1		*anthrópos*	Let a man so consider us, as servants
4:9		*anthrópois*	apostles, last, as men condemned to
6:18		*anthrópos*	Every sin that a man does is outside
7:1		*anthrópó*	*It is* good for a man not to touch
7:7		*anthrópous*	I wish that all men were even as I myself
7:23		*anthrópón*	do not become slaves of men
7:26		*anthrópó*	*it is* good for a man to remain as he is
9:8		*anthrópon*	I say these things as a *mere* man
11:28		*anthrópos*	But let a man examine himself, and so let
13:1	*tón*	*anthrópón*	I speak with the tongues of men and of angels
14:2		*anthrópois*	does not speak to men but to God
14:3		*anthrópois*	edification and exhortation and comfort to men
15:19		*anthrópón*	we are of all men the most pitiable

	15:21	*anthrópou*	For since by man *came* death
	15:21	*anthrópou*	by Man also *came* the resurrection of the dead
	15:32	*anthrópon*	If, in the manner of men, I have fought
	15:39	*anthrópón*	flesh of men, another flesh of beasts, another of
	15:45 ho	*anthrópos*	*The first man Adam became a living being*
	15:47 ho	*anthrópos*	The first man *was* of the earth, *made* of dust
	15:47 ho	*anthrópos*	the second Man *is* the Lord from heaven
2 Corinthians	3:2	*anthrópón*	known and read by all men
	4:2	*anthrópón*	commending ourselves to every man's conscience
	4:16 ho	*anthrópos*	Even though our outward man is perishing
	5:11	*anthrópous*	we persuade men; but we are well known
	8:21	*anthrópón*	but also in the sight of men
	12:2	*anthrópon*	I know a man in Christ who fourteen years ago
	12:3 ton	*anthrópon*	And I know such a man
	12:4	*anthrópó*	it is not lawful for a man to utter
Galatians	1:1	*anthrópón*	PAUL, an apostle (not from men
	1:1	*anthrópou*	nor through man, but through Jesus Christ
	1:10	*anthrópous*	For do I now persuade men, or God?
	1:10	*anthrópois*	Or do I seek to please men?
	1:10	*anthrópois*	For if I still pleased men, I would not
	1:11	*anthrópon*	preached by me is not according to man
	1:12	*anthrópou*	For I neither received it from man, nor was I

	2:6	*anthrópou*	God shows personal favouritism to no man
	2:16	*anthrópos*	knowing that a man is not justified by the works
	3:12 *ho*	*anthrópos*	*The man who does them shall live by them*
	3:15	*anthrópon*	Brethren, I speak in the manner of men
	3:15	*anthrópou*	Though *it is* only a man's covenant
	5:3	*anthrópó*	I testify again to every man who becomes
	6:1	*anthrópos*	Brethren, if a man is overtaken in any trespass
	6:7	*anthrópos*	for whatever a man sows, that he will also reap
Ephesians	2:15	*anthrópon*	create in Himself one new man *from* the two
	3:5 *tón*	*anthrópón*	made known to the sons of men
	3:16 *ton*	*anthrópon*	through His Spirit in the inner man
	4:8 *tois*	*anthrópois*	*And gave gifts to men*
	4:14 *tón*	*anthrópón*	by the trickery of men, in the cunning
	4:22 *ton*	*anthrópon*	the old man which grows corrupt according to
	4:24 *ton*	*anthrópon*	that you put on the new man which was created
	5:31	*anthrópos*	*For this reason a man shall leave his father*
	6:7	*anthrópois*	service, as to the Lord, and not to men
Philippians	2:7	*anthrópón*	*and* coming in the likeness of men
	2:8	*anthrópos*	being found in appearance as a man
	4:5	*anthrópois*	Let your gentleness be known to all men

Colossians	1:28		*anthrópon*	we preach, warning every man
	1:28		*anthrópon*	and teaching every man in all wisdom
	1:28		*anthrópon*	that we may present every man perfect
	2:8	*tón*	*anthrópón*	according to the traditions of men
	2:22	*tón*	*anthrópón*	the commandments and doctrines of men
	3:9	*ton*	*anthrópon*	put off the old man with his deeds
	3:23		*anthrópois*	as to the Lord and not to men
1 Thessalonians	2:4		*anthrópois*	we speak, not as pleasing to men, but God
	2:6		*anthrópón*	Nor did we seek glory from men
	2:13		*anthrópón*	not *as* the word of men, but as it is in truth
	2:15		*anthrópois*	do not please God and are contrary to all men
	4:8		*anthrópon*	does not reject man, but God, who has also
2 Thessalonians	2:3	*ho*	*anthrópos*	and the man of sin is revealed, the son of
	3:2	*tón*	*anthrópón*	from unreasonable and wicked men
1 Timothy	2:1		*anthrópón*	*and* giving of thanks be made for all men
	2:4		*anthrópous*	who desires all men to be saved
	2:5		*anthrópón*	one Mediator between God and men
	2:5		*anthrópos*	*the* Man Christ Jesus
	4:10		*anthrópón*	who is *the* Saviour of all men, especially
	5:24		*anthrópón*	Some men's sins are clearly evident, preceding

	6:5		*anthrópón*	useless wranglings of men of corrupt minds
	6:9	*tous*	*anthrópous*	lusts which drown men in destruction
	6:11		*anthrópe*	But you, O man of God, flee these things
	6:16		*anthrópón*	unapproachable light, whom no man has seen
2 Timothy	2:2		*anthrópois*	commit these to faithful men who will be able
	3:2	*hoi*	*anthrópoi*	For men will be lovers of themselves
	3:8		*anthrópoi*	men of corrupt minds, disapproved concerning
	3:13		*anthrópoi*	But evil men and impostors will grow worse
	3:17	*ho*	*anthrópos*	that the man of God may be complete, thoroughly
Titus	1:14		*anthrópón*	fables and commandments of men who turn from
	2:11		*anthrópois*	that brings salvation has appeared to all men
	3:2		*anthrópous*	showing all humility to all men
	3:8	*tois*	*anthrópois*	These things are good and profitable to men
	3:10		*anthrópon*	Reject a divisive man after the first and second
Hebrews	2:6		*anthrópos*	*What is man that You are mindful of him*
	2:6		*anthrópou*	*Or the son of man that you take care of him*
	5:1		*anthrópón*	every high priest taken from among men
	5:1		*anthrópón*	is appointed for men in things *pertaining* to God
	6:16		*anthrópoi*	For men indeed swear by the greater, and an oath
	7:8		*anthrópoi*	Here mortal men receive tithes, but there

	7:28		*anthrópous*	appoints as high priests men who have weakness
	8:2		*anthrópos*	which the Lord erected, and not man
	9:27	*tois*	*anthrópois*	it is appointed for men to die once, but after
	13:6		*anthrópos*	*I will not fear. What can man do to me?*
James	1:7	*ho*	*anthrópos*	For let not that man suppose that he will
	1:19		*anthrópos*	let every man be swift to hear, slow to speak
	2:20		*anthrópe*	do you want to know, O foolish man, that faith
	2:24		*anthrópos*	You see then that a man is justified by works
	3:8		*anthrópón*	But no man can tame the tongue
	3:9	*tous*	*anthrópous*	and with it we curse men, who have been made
	5:17		*anthrópos*	Elijah was a man with a nature like ours
1 Peter	1:24		*anthrópou*	*all the glory of man as the flower of the grass*
	2:4		*anthrópón*	rejected indeed by men, but chosen by God
	2:15	*tón*	*anthrópón*	put to silence the ignorance of foolish men
	3:4		*anthrópos*	*let it be* the hidden person of the heart, with the [But *let it be* the hidden man of the heart, in that which is not corruptible KJV]
	4:2		*anthrópón*	for the lusts of men, but for the will of God
	4:6		*anthrópous*	judged according to men in the flesh, but live
2 Peter	1:21		*anthrópou*	prophecy never came by the will of man

	1:21		*anthrópoi*	but holy men of God spoke *as they were* moved
	2:16		*anthrópou*	a dumb donkey speaking with a man's voice
	3:7	*tón*	*anthrópon*	judgment and perdition of ungodly men
1 John	5:9	*tón*	*anthrópon*	If we receive the witness of men, the witness of God
Jude	4		*anthrópoi*	For certain men have crept in unnoticed
Revelation	1:13		***anthrópou***	*One* like **the Son of Man**, clothed with a garment
	4:7		*anthrópos*	the third living creature had a face like a man
	8:11		*anthrópon*	and many men died from the water, because
	9:4	*tous*	*anthrópous*	but only those men who do not have the seal
	9:5		*anthrópon*	the torment of a scorpion when it strikes a man
	9:6	*hoi*	*anthrópoi*	In those days men will seek death
	9:7		*anthrópon*	their faces *were* like the faces of men
	9:10	*tous*	*anthrópous*	their power *was* to hurt men five months
	9:15	*tón*	*anthrópon*	were released to kill a third of mankind
	9:18	*tón*	*anthrópon*	a third of mankind was killed- by the fire and the
	9:20	*tón*	*anthrópon*	But the rest of mankind, who were not killed
	11:13		*anthrópon*	In the earthquake seven thousand men were killed
	13:13	*tón*	*anthrópon*	from heaven on the earth in the sight of men
	13:18		*anthrópou*	for it is the number of a man: His number is 666
	14:4	*tón*	*anthrópon*	were redeemed from *among* men, *being* firstfruits

16:2	*tous*	*anthrópous*	sore came upon the men who had the mark
16:8	*tous*	*anthrópous*	power was given to him to scorch men with fire
16:9	*hoi*	*anthrópoi*	And men were scorched with great heat
16:18	*hoi*	*anthrópoi*	as had not occurred since men were on the earth
16:21	*tous*	*anthrópous*	great hail from heaven fell upon men
16:21	*hoi*	*anthrópoi*	And men blasphemed God because of the plague
18:13		*anthrópón*	and chariots, and bodies and souls of men
21:3	*tón*	*anthrópón*	the tabernacle of God *is* with men, and He will dwell
21:17		*anthrópou*	*according* to the measure of a man, that is,

APPENDIX 6

PROTHESIS

This appendix serves as added information to back up the translation of Romans 8:28 in chapter 11.

> But we know that to the ones loving God He works together all into good, for they are the ones called according to a displayed intent. *Romans 8:28 JM*

The Septuagint (LXX) is the Greek version of the Old Testament scriptures. As found in the New Testament it is the text from which Paul and the other apostles often quoted. It is useful here in helping highlight the meaning of this Greek word found in the New Testament. Since this Greek is the same as used in the New Testament and the authors knew it, the Septuagint is a valuable tool to help ascertain meanings to words. The inspiration of the Septuagint text is not being queried, it is not an issue; the use of the words in the Greek are. And Koïne Greek, as the New Testament Greek is known, has precious few examples of the language in the written records such that to have one such example as the Septuagint, also known and valued by the Lord and the apostles, makes it important and of value to take note of. See Chapter 3 for examples of New Testament quotes of the Septuagint.

The Greek word *prothesis* sometimes translated as "purpose" is accurately also understood as "a display" (i.e. an observed intent of the heart) since its uses in the Septuagint shows it as separate and distinct from the words *artos* (bread) and *trapedza* (table) in reference to the shewbread or, the table of the shewbread.

To help show this I now quote every reference for *prothesis* in the Septuagint and give a breakdown of the Greek to show the validity of "a setting forth", "a displayed intent" as a good meaning for *prothesis*.

The following passages are dealt with:

Exodus 39:18	1 Chronicles 28:16
Exodus 40:4	2 Chronicles 2:4
Exodus 40:23	2 Chronicles 4:19
1 Samuel 21:6	2 Chronicles 13:11
1 Chronicles 9:32	2 Chronicles 29:18
1 Chronicles 23:29	

Throughout the following passages *trapedza* = table and *artos* = bread (these are not in dispute), *prothesis* is however not so well recognised in the New Testament usage as "a setting forth" or, "a displayed intent" as I have translated it, but "a purpose". As per the note in the introduction, "ó" = *omega* and, "é" = *éta*.

Exodus 39:18
(N.B. Exodus 39:37-41 in our translations from the Hebrew is the area, but this passage is not included)

> *Kai tén <u>trapedzan</u> tés **protheseós**,*
> and the <u>table</u> of **shewbread**,

> *Kai - tén - <u>trapedzan</u> - tés - **protheseós**,*
> and - the - <u>table</u> - of the - **(of) showings**,

> *protheseós* = (of) showings [bread is only implied and thereby is understood as the shew-bread]

Exodus 40:4

> *Kai eisoiseis tén <u>trapedzan</u>, kai **prothéseis** tén **prothesin** autés*
> and thou shalt bring in the <u>table</u> and **shalt set forth**[1] that which is **to be set forth** on it;

*kai - eisoiseis - tén - <u>trapedzan</u>, * kai - **prothéseis** - tén
- **prothesin** - autés*
and - you shall bring - the - <u>table</u>, * and - **(he) shall set
forth** - the - **(a) setting forth** - of her;

protheseis = he shall set forth [hence the translator's
note: "Setting forth of it"] *prothesin* = to be set forth - [the]
showing - [the] display

[1]"Setting forth of it"

Exodus 40:23

*Kai prosethéken ep' autés <u>artous</u> tés **protheseós** enanti
Kuriou,*
And he put on it the **shewbread** before the Lord,

*Kai - prosethéken - ep' - autés - <u>artous</u> - tés - **protheseós**
- enanti - Kuriou,*
And - he put forth - upon - of her - <u>breads</u> - of the - **(of)
showings** - before - [the] Lord,

protheseós = (of) showings [unlike Exodus 39:18 the
implication of bread is removed by stating "bread" explicitly:
thus shows *prothesis* on it's own as a showing - a display]

1 Samuel 21:6

*Kai edóken autó Abimelech ho hiereus tous <u>artous</u>
tés **protheseós**, hoti ekei ouk én artoi, all' é artoi tou
prosópou hoi aphérémenoi ek prosópou Kuriou,*
So Abimelech the priest gave him the **shewbread**; for
there were no loaves there, but only the presence loaves
which had been removed from the presence of the Lord,

Kai - edóken - autó - Abimelech - ho - hiereus - tous -
<u>*artous*</u> *- tés -* **protheseós**, * *hoti - ekei - ouk - én - artoi,*
* *all' - é - artoi - tou - prosópou - hoi - aphérémenoi - ek*
- prosópou - Kuriou,

And/So - (he) gave - to/for him - Abimelech - the - priest -
the - <u>bread(s)</u> - of the - **(of) showings**, * since/due to -
there - no - was - breads, * but - (was) - breads - of the - (of)
face [i.e. presence] - the - had been removed(s) - out of/from
- (of) face [presence] - of [the] Lord,

protheseós = of showings [Just like Exodus 40:23, but
unlike Exodus 39:18 the implication of bread is removed by
stating "bread" explicitly: this shows *prothesis* on it's own
as: a showing - a display]

1 Chronicles 9:32

Kai Banaias ho kaathités ek tón adelphón autón epi tón <u>*artón*</u>
tés **protheseós**, *tou etoimasai sabbatón kata sabbaton.*
And Banaias the Caathite, from among their brethren, *was
set* over the **shewbread**, to prepare it every sabbath.

Kai - Banaias - ho - kaathités - ek - tón - adelphón -
autón - epi - tón - <u>*artón*</u> *- tés -* **protheseós**, * *tou -*
etoimasai - sabbatón - kata - sabbaton.
And - Banaias - the - Caathite - out of/from - of the - (of)
brothers - of them/their - upon - the - <u>breads</u> - of the - **(of)
showings**, * of the - preparing - of sabbaths - according to
- sabbath.

protheseós = of showings [as per 1 Samuel 21:6]

1 Chronicles 23:29

*kai eis tous <u>artous</u> tés **protheseós**, kai eis tén semidalin
tés thusias, kai eis ta lagana ta adzuma,*
and for the **shew-bread**, and for the fine flour of the
meat-offering, and for the unleavened cakes,

*kai - eis - tous - <u>artous</u> - tés – **protheseós**, * kai - eis -
tén - semidalin - tés - thusias, * kai - eis - ta - lagana -
ta - adzuma,*
and - into/to [for] - the - <u>breads</u> - of the - **(of) showings**,
* and - into/to [for] - the - fine flour - of the - (of) sacrifice,
* and - into/to [for] - the - cakes - the - unleavened,

protheseós = of showings [as per 1 Samuel 21:6]

1 Chronicles 28:16

*Edóken autó homoiós ton stathmon tón <u>trapedzón</u> tés
protheseós, ekastés trapedzés chrusés,*
He gave him likewise the weight of the <u>tables</u> of **shewbread**[1],
of each table of gold,

*Edóken - autó - homoiós - ton - stathmon - tón - <u>trapedzón</u>
- tés - **protheseós**, * ekastés - trapedzés - chrusés,*
He gave - (to/for) him - like - the - weight - of the - <u>(of) tables</u>
- of the - **(of) showings**, * of each - (of) table - (of) gold,

protheseós = (of) showings/ setting forth [As per Exodus
39:18]

[1]Gr. tables of the setting forth

2 Chronicles 2:4

> *hagiasai auton autó tou thumian apenanti autou*
> *thumiama kai* **prothesin** *diapantos, kai tou anapherein*
> *holokautómata diapantos toprói kai todeilés,*
> to consecrate it to him, to burn incense before him, and
> *to offer* **shewbread** continually, and to offer up whole-
> burnt-offerings continually morning and evening,

> *hagiasai - auton - autó - tou - thumian - apenanti - autou*
> *- thumiama - kai -* **prothesin** *- diapantos,* * *kai - tou -*
> *anapherein - holokautómata - diapantos - toprói - kai -*
> *todeilés,*
> to consecrate - it - to/for him - of the - incense - before - of
> him/his - incense - and - **a showing** - continually/always
> by, * and - of the - to offer up - whole-burnt-offerings -
> continually/always by - the dawnings - and - the settings,

> *prothesin* = a showing, a setting forth [As per Exodus
> 39:18]

2 Chronicles 4:19

> *Kai epoiése Salómón panta ta skeué oikou Kuriou, kai to*
> *thusiastérion to chrusoun, kai tas <u>trapedzas</u>, kai ep'*
> *autón artoi* **protheseós,**
> And Solomon made all the vessels of the house of the Lord,
> and the golden altar, and the <u>tables</u>, and upon them *were to*
> *be* the <u>loaves</u> of **shewbread**;

> *Kai - epoiése - Salómón - panta - ta - skeué - oikou -*
> *Kuriou - kai - to - thusiastérion - to - chrusoun,* * *kai -*
> *tas - <u>trapedzas</u> - kai - ep' - autón - <u>artoi</u> -* **protheseós,**

And - he made - Solomon - all - the - vessel - of house - of
[the] Lord - and - the - altar - the - golden, * and - the -
<u>tables</u> - and - upon - of them - <u>breads</u> - ***of* showings**,

protheseós = of showings/ of setting forths [as per 1 Samuel
21:6]

2 Chronicles 13:11

*kai thumiama suntheseós, kai **protheseis** <u>artón</u> epi tés
trapedzés tés katharas,*
and compound incense, and *set* the **shewbread** on the
pure table;

*kai - thumiama - suntheseós, * kai - **protheseis** -
<u>artón</u> - epi - tés - trapedzés - tés - katharas,*
and - incence - compound, * and - **showed** - <u>of breads</u> -
upon - of the - (of) table - of the - (of) pure,

protheseis = showed [the implication of bread is removed by
stating "breads" explicitly: this shows *prothesis* on it's own
as: a showing - a display - a setting forth (i.e. an intent seen,
a purpose visualised in the context of Romans 8:28)]

2 Chronicles 29:18

*to thusiastérion tés holokautóseós kai ta skeué autou, kai
tén <u>trapedzan</u> tés **protheseós** kai ta skeué autés,*
the altar of whole-burnt-offering, and its vessels, and the
<u>table</u> of **shew-bread**, and its vessels;

*to - thusiastérion - tés - holokautóseós - kai - ta - skeué -
autou, * kai - tén - <u>trapedzan</u> - tés - **protheseós** - kai -
ta - skeué - autés,*

the - altar - of the - (of) whole-burnt-offerings - and - the - vessel - of it, * and - the - <u>table</u> - of the - **(of) showings** - and - the - vessel - of her,

protheseós = (of) showings/ setting forths [As per Exodus 39:18]

Both Greek words and the initial translation quoted are taken from *The Septuagint with Apocrypha: Greek and English* by Sir Lancelot C.L. Brenton and published by Hendrikson Publishers, Peabody, MA. Originally published in 1851 by Samuel Bagster & Sons Ltd, London.

Conclusion

Prothesis on it's own due to the context of the Old Testament Septuagint passages is seen to mean "the shewbread". That is, the loaves of bread which were put on a table for a symbol before the Lord in the temple. But when the word for bread – *artos* is added it still means just the same. This tells us that the word *prothesis* itself is understood to mean "a showing" or "a display". In it's common use in the New Testament as "purpose" it can thereby be also understood as a "display of intent" - "a plan in view" which is in fact an equivalent meaning for the word "purpose" itself. A "setting forth", a "showing" appears to be the core meaning with *Pro* – "in front of" and *thesis* – "a view of (mental or otherwise)", such that if mental it is an idea or theory, a plan or decided aim, a purpose – a display of intent:

Romans 8:28 – God who searches the heart (Psalm 7:9; Jeremiah 17:10; Revelation 2:23), by His Spirit intercedes and then sets the individual up – predestines (as per Romans 8:26-30) – to a calling following a display of love witnessed in the heart: for "**as many as received Him, to them He gave the right to become children of God**" (John 1:12).

AUTHENTEÓ

*A**utheneó* is one of the Greek verbs which occurs in 1 Timothy 2:12. Because this verb is not found elsewhere in the New Testament it requires attention into ascertaining it's meaning. This is especially true since 1 Timothy 2:12 is one of the 3 main texts which has caused much influence on the issue of women in leadership. In the NKJV we find:

> And I do not permit a woman to teach or to have authority over a man, but to be in silence.   *1 Timothy 2:12*

As per chapter 13 I explain my translation as follows:

> And I do not allow for a woman to teach, nor to exercise authority of a husband, but to be in quietness.
>
> *1 Timothy 2:12 JM*

In the NKJV we read the verb *authenteó* in it's Infinitive form *authentein* translated as, "to have authority". The next good place to look for the use of a Greek word is the Septuagint since, as a text it was used by the apostles and Jesus: they all quoted directly from it. This is the Greek Version of the Old Testament Hebrew Scripture which was translated about 285-247BC. I expand a little more on this in Chapter 3. However, here also the word was not used. And so the fun begins. The places where it is found are thereby extra-biblical in nature, but the interpretation of it's meaning are heavily dependent on the view of the researcher. This can be seen from the 2 main researches I have read on this matter. The one attributes to *authenteó* an understanding of "overbearing rule" a "usurping authority" whilst the other just a plain "exercise of authority", "to have authority" (as in the NKJV) without any taste of negative or overbearing pressure.

So, that what I wish to do with this appendix is review these 2 views and thereby end with the most likely of the two's meaning for *authenteó*.

The two researches in question are George W. Knight III's *Authenteó in reference to women in 1 Timothy 2.12* published in *New Testament Studies* Vol. 30 pp. 143–157 and, Catherine C. Kroeger's *Ancient heresies and a strange Greek verb* published in *The Reformed Journal* March 1979 pp. 12-15.

Under the fair dealings provisions of the 1988 Copyright Act one may do reviews of works and this is the way in which I intend to use their material.

The interest in Kroeger's work comes from writers for women in leadership. Her conclusions are that the word refers to an over-bearing rule. It has a negative emphasis with a sexual overtone. With this understanding it is used to give a picture of a type of authority which Paul advocates women should not use and thereby remove any implication of any other types of "rule". However, as I looked and studied her paper I counted about 19 direct sources for the noun similar in form to *authenteó*, but not for the verb itself. Though when I say sources only about 5 were given an actual source reference; the rest were just mentioned without. As to the verb, Kroeger makes reference to only two direct sources, but again without the means of checking the place of origin: Reference is made to Philodemus and the Byzantine Michael Glycas. There is no other direct source reference to the verb. There are also two indirect sources. To lay so much weight on the meaning of the noun which has a similar form to *authenteó* in order to suggest what the verb means is dependent on how close they are in meaning. This is not automatic since there are verbs which are similar in meaning to the nouns which have a similar look and then there are those with completely different meanings or emphasis. To base the view of one upon the other is possible, but not necessarily accurate methodology. To give examples of this in English: "to chair" as a verb has to do with directing or overseeing a group of people like in a committee, but "a chair" as a noun is a piece of furniture you sit on. The meaning of the noun is very different to the verb though the form is similar no matter how many examples you give of the noun it bears no resemblance to the verb in meaning. That is an example at one extreme. Another probably closer to the Kroeger "formula" is that of the verb "to need" compared with the adjective "needy". I may need advice about something, but no amount of "needy" emphasising a poor or destitute person will wholly show the truth about the verb "to need" in the context I gave. And, at the other extreme end of the comparison scale the verb "to help" is very close in meaning to the noun "helper". Suffice to say I have raised enough doubt on Kroeger's work here to show the methodology alone is unhelpful.

Knight's research on the other hand offers not only 10 direct sources for the verb and it's accompanying place of origin so any one can check it out, but of his quotes of Philodemus in *Rhetorica* (1st Century BC) to mean "those in authority" (they that rule) and Michael Glycas in his *Annals* (12th Century AD) to mean "to have your own power (authority)" there is clear variance from Kroeger's reading from them. Knight having compared all the 10 sources and used others' translations of these rather than his own so as not to influence the understanding, his conclusion that *authenteó* be placed as a word in the realm of authority, in the objective and neutral sense with the most commonly suggested meaning of "have authority over" appears to be on somewhat much firmer evidence of a direct kind than anything Kroeger offers. Knight's list of sources came from Bauer, Arndt, Gingrich and Danker's *Greek-English Lexicon of the New Testament and Other Early Christian Literature* plus a few more. These are claimed as more comprehensive and fuller for a meaning source as a whole than offered by Thayer's *Greek-English Lexicon*. He closes by saying the RSV, NAB, NIV and The Translator's Testament have caught the essence of the meaning of *authenteó* and present probably the most satisfactory rendering with their phrase "**to have authority**".

Of course this meaning or any meaning if not taking into account that the next word is in the Genitive as explained in Chapter Thirteen, profoundly changes the outcome of the use of this alleged meaning. Kroeger's becomes completely ineffective as an argument, whilst Knight's makes full sense if one then looks at what type of authority a husband has been given at the beginning in regards to the one flesh relationship.

LIST OF BIBLE PASSAGES ADDRESSED

What happens to those who do not hear?
The man born deaf and blind?
The righteous in the bible are not just those
known as Christians

The issue of women in leadership
Without deception understood no book deals with it.
This one does!

So You Think You're
CH✚SEN?

Jacques More

J_{ar}Bo

A comprehensive response to Calvinism
A look at the 5th century doctrine against the bible
Paul's conditional predestination explained

REVIVAL
THE BATTLEPLAN

by Jacques More

A vision of how it could happen
The part the youth can play
The Church working together is the way forward